Contents

Introduction

There is a brighter side to Peterborough's history, with all manner of unbelievable events that have occurred here, from the local boy who ended up working on the Large Hadron Collider to the sweet smell of success by a self-made confectionery manufacturer. Londoners have flocked to our city, and Peterborough has welcomed refugees since the Huguenots arrived and continues to welcome them to this day. We are one of the UK's fastest-growing cities. Why? Well, the word gets around that we are inclusive, that new estates are beautifully laid out and good places to live, plus it's a commuter's paradise, with good links in every direction.

Peterborough boasts a significant historical background, dating back 3,500 years to the Bronze Age. The city is distinguished by its cultural diversity, accommodating various nationalities and fostering an inclusive and welcoming environment. Additionally, Peterborough offers more affordable housing compared to London and Cambridge.

Peterborough City Council was one of the first to adopt an Environmental Charter, to promote conservation and better use of natural resources while reducing pollution.

The city has various stories and historical facts, some of which are unusual but true. The 2021 census data indicates that there is a high proportion of individuals under fifteen years old, with one in five falling into this age group. This demographic trend is seen as beneficial for future development.

Peterborough is modern but it also has a good sense of its past. This book provides a look at the quirky aspects of its history, highlighting notable individuals, significant events and traditions, as well as unique locations associated with our city.

Local Boy Achieves Outstanding Success

Mike Sendall, born on 7 October 1939 in Peterborough, attended King's School where he was a prefect. He joined CERN in Geneva and became Secretary of the Large Hadron Collider Experiments Committee. The Large Hadron Collider is the world's largest and most powerful particle accelerator, spanning 27 kilometres with superconducting magnets.

Though a broad range of subjects interested him deeply, in 1958 he went to Trinity College, Cambridge, to read physics and chemistry. In 1965, he obtained his PhD at the Cavendish Laboratory under Otto Frisch, working on an assortment of remarkable gadgets invented to analyse photographs of particle collisions taken using detectors called bubble chambers. It was during this

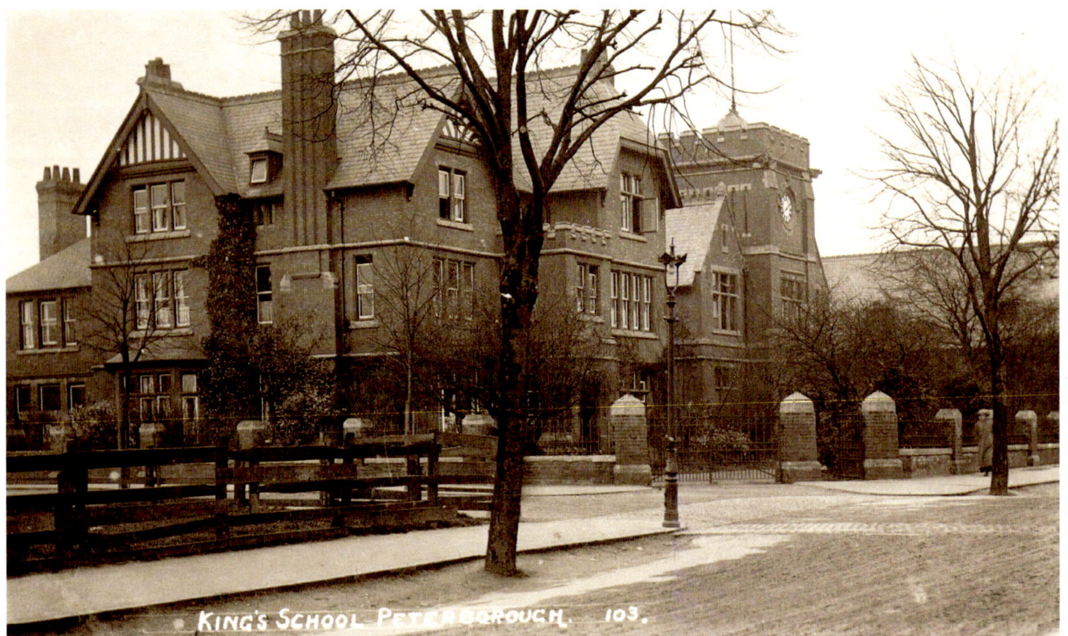

King's School, Park Road, *c.* 1910.

period, while programming the Electronic Delay Storage Automatic Calculator (EDSAC) and other early calculating engines, that he developed his fascination for computers.

From 1972 onwards Mike devoted much of his career to the design, implementation, and operation of computer-based systems for data collection from the increasingly complex detectors being exploited at CERN's particle accelerators. His open and unassuming personality, never seeking credit for himself, made him an ideal adviser and supervisor.

The stage was being set for the invention of the World Wide Web, and future history books will recount how, almost alone, Mike Sendall supported the pioneering work of Tim Berners-Lee, then working in his group. After reading Berners-Lee's prophetic 1989 proposal for what would become the web, Sendall wrote on the cover, 'Vague but exciting', adding at the end, 'And now?' The rest is history.

In 1992, Mike took on the important responsibility of secretary of CERN's Large Hadron Collider Experiments Committee, set up to recommend which experiments should be approved and to monitor the subsequent development and progress of them. He approached this role with meticulous diligence.

Mike's modesty hid a much deeper intellect; he was a polymath in the classic English mould. He had a refined sense of humour, making him an exceptional storyteller who could engage an audience or contribute to scholarly discussions with his characteristic gentleness.

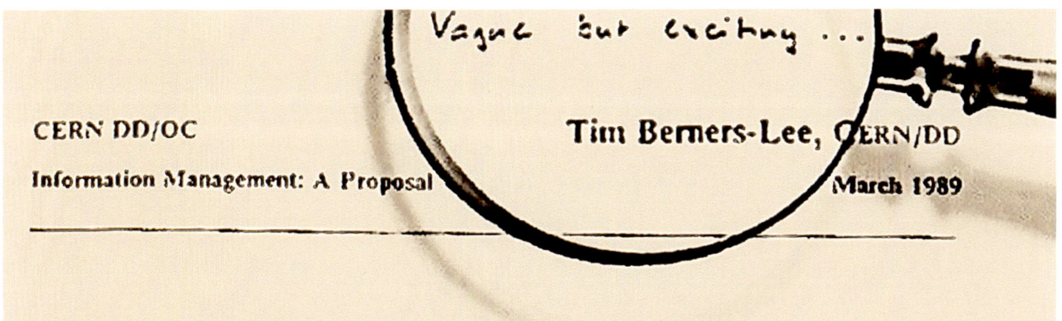

Information Management: A Proposal

Abstract

This proposal concerns the management of general information about accelerators and experiments at CERN. It discusses the problems of loss of information about complex evolving systems and derives a solution based on a distributed hypertext sytstem.

Keywords: Hypertext, Computer conferencing, Document retrieval, Information management, Project control

World Wide Web inventor Tim Berners-Lee's proposal to his boss, Mike Sendall.

In 1989, Mike was diagnosed as having multiple myeloma, a form of bone marrow cancer. He faced the situation with courage and dignity, living a full life until the very end. He was lovingly supported by Dr Elsie (Peggie) Rimmer, his constant friend and companion for thirty years. They eventually married in 1990. Mike fully acknowledged what was happening to his body while playing down the impact and inconvenience. He spent his last hours watching a television broadcast in Arabic to refresh his knowledge of that language. He died in London on 15 July 1999.

Clay Pipe Alice

Alice McKenzie (born around 1849) was raised in Peterborough and moved to the East End of London in 1874. McKenzie was known as 'Clay Pipe Alice' owing to her pipe-smoking habit. She was a long-term resident of a lodging house in Gun Street, Spitalfields, with her partner, John McCormack, a tailor's porter. As well as working as a charwoman, she also worked the streets on occasion as a prostitute. Alice is believed to have been an only child, and she had a son who emigrated to America. Her father was a postman in Liverpool, but she was estranged from her family.

According to Dr Thomas Bond, a surgeon and first offender profiler, Alice was murdered by Jack the Ripper on 17 July 1889. Alice's body was found in Castle Alley at 12.50 a.m. on Wednesday 17 July. In her possession was a clay pipe and a farthing. She was found by a policeman and her body was taken to the mortuary

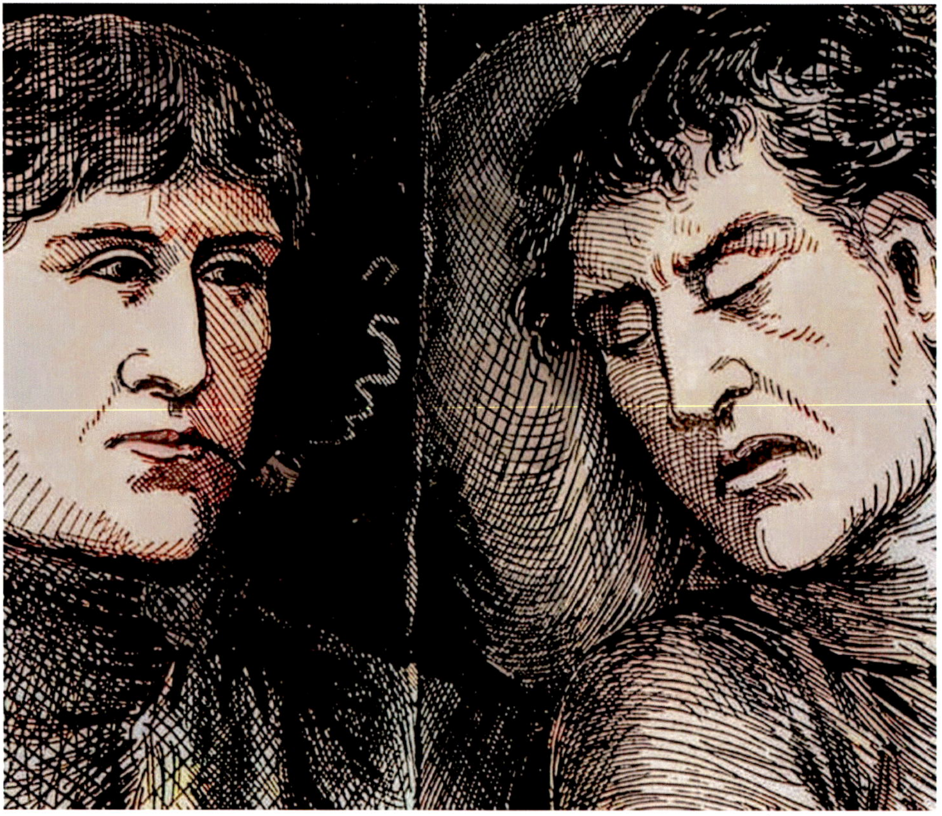

Illustrated Police News image of McKenzie, 27 July 1889.

where, under examination, she was found to have eight injuries caused by a sharp pointed weapon:

- Cause of death due to severance of the left carotid artery
- Two stabs in the left side of the neck carried forward in the same skin wound
- Some bruising on chest
- Five bruises or marks on left side of abdomen
- Cut was made from left to right, apparently while Alice was on the ground
- A long 7-inch 'but not unduly deep' wound from the bottom of her breast to the navel
- Seven or eight scratches beginning at the navel and pointing towards the genitalia
- Small cut across the *mons veneris* (fatty tissue that covers the pubic bone)

According to eyewitness the murder was thought to have occurred between 12.25 a.m. and 12.50 a.m. It is thought that Jack the Ripper was interrupted in his murderous deed, so the injuries were not as deep and sustained as previous victims.

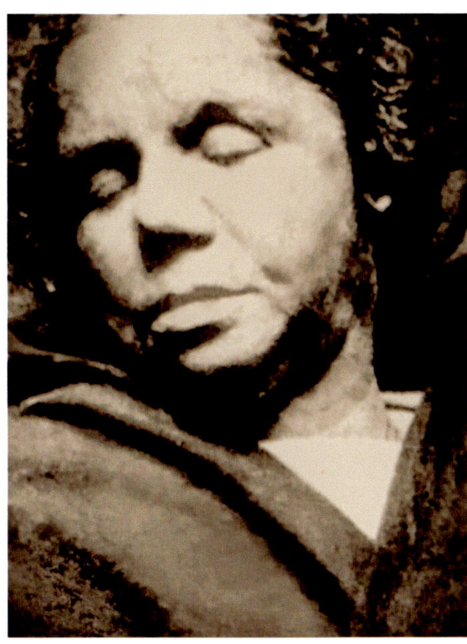

Mortuary image of Alice McKenzie.

A Russian con artist, a Polish barber, an Irish-American quack and even the eldest son of Edward VII are just some who have been considered for being Jack the Ripper – the man who brought terror to the heart of London's East End before disappearing without a trace. The Ripper's identity has been a point of considerable speculation for over a century.

A twenty-three-year-old Polish barber named Aaron Kosminski was a suspect at the time of the murders, but police were unable to arrest him as they had no proof of his involvement – that is, until now. A bloodstained shawl said to have been found at the body of one of the victims was purchased at auction in 2007 by author and researcher Russell Edwards. It was found to have the DNA of both a victim and Kosminski.

In October 2024, Russell Edwards revealed that Kosminski's connections to Freemasons might have protected him from the law and led to his confinement in an asylum, where he eventually died.

Kosminski's oldest brother's great-great-granddaughter provided a DNA sample that matched with the victim's shawl, helping Edwards identify the killer.

During the original inquest on 4 October 1888, the verdict was wilful murder. At that time, police were still searching for the serial killer.

Sweet Street

Westgate was where 'the Rock King', James Arthur Lewin, born to a Peakirk shoemaker in 1868, had his sweet stall. The man with the Stetson, wearing a pink carnation in his jacket buttonhole, sold vast quantities of rock, nougat and sweetmeats from his stall. James worked the land before joining Richardson's, a local sugar-boiling business, and from there he branched out to make his own confectionery at the age of nineteen.

In addition to staffing his stall in Westgate, Peterborough, he also toured across the east of England, selling his wares at markets. James was highly popular with local children, who would rush to the stall on his arrival as he was renowned for his generosity in giving away sweets to the young ones.

This larger-than-life character lived on Garton End Road for years before moving to Daisy House on Brook Street. James died in January 1942 shortly after

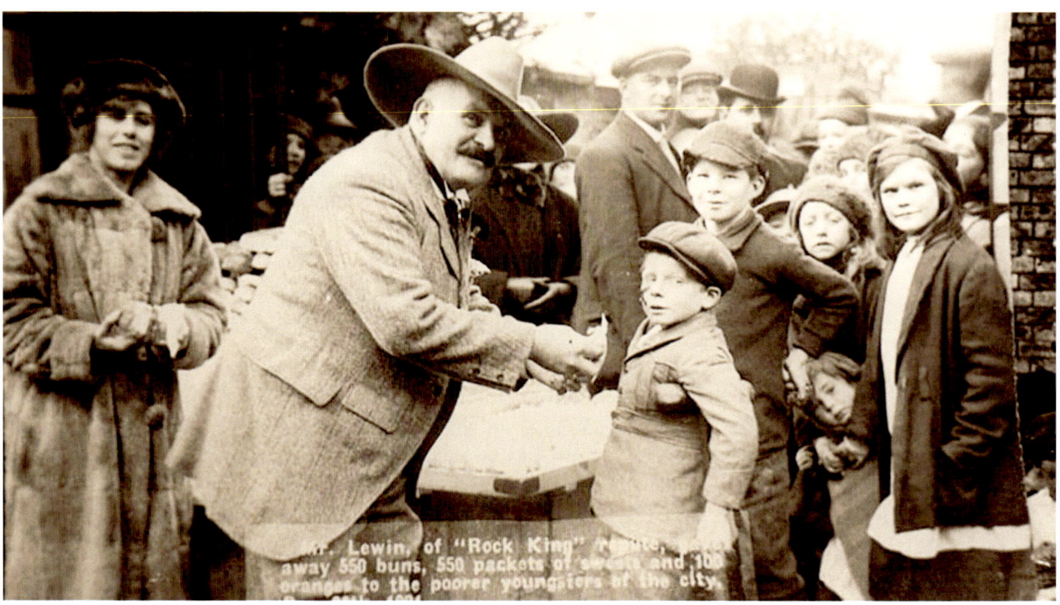

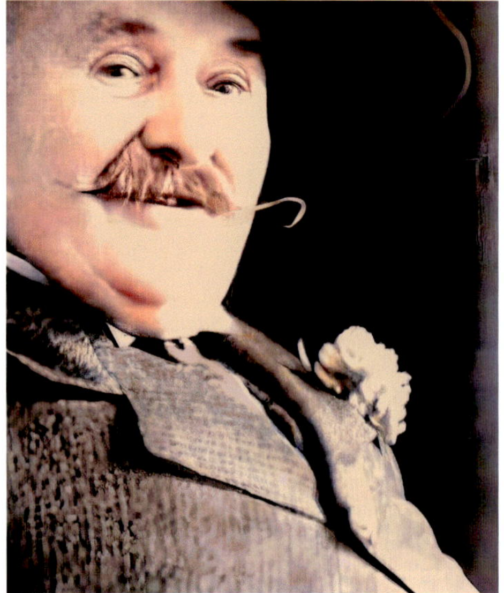

Above: The Rock King giving out buns and sweets.

Left: James Lewin, known as the Rock King.

Opposite above: James Lewin and an array of his sweets and treats, *c.* 1908.

Opposite below: The Rock King's stall, *c.* 1920.

celebrating his golden wedding anniversary with his wife, Elizabeth, with whom he had ten children.

His son, James Arthur Jnr, continued the business from his home at Mead Close, Walton, until 1951 before deciding to work at Peter Brotherhoods as it offered a better income.

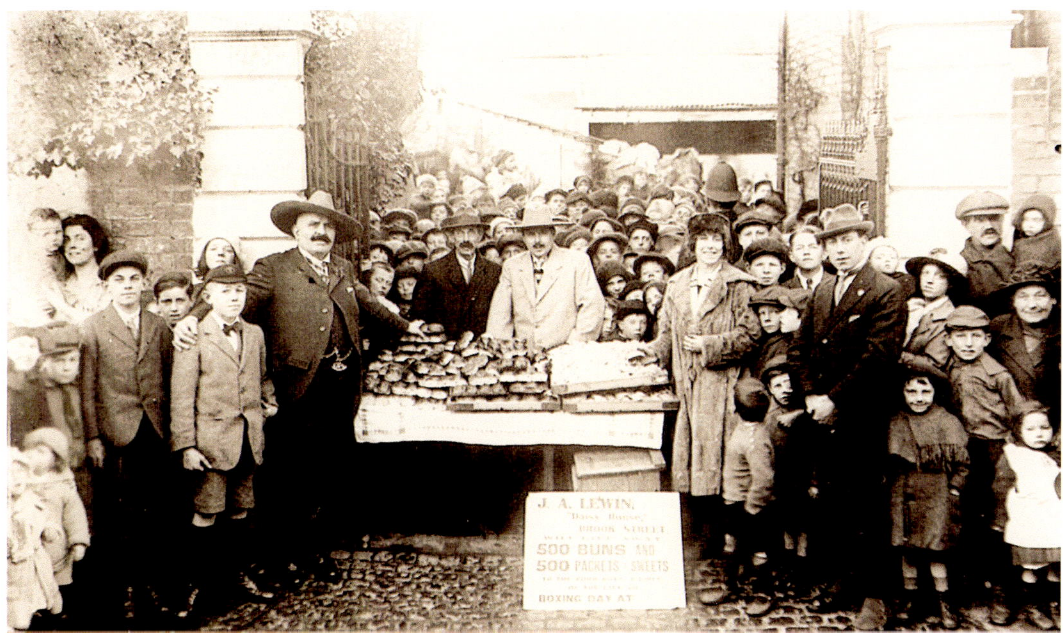

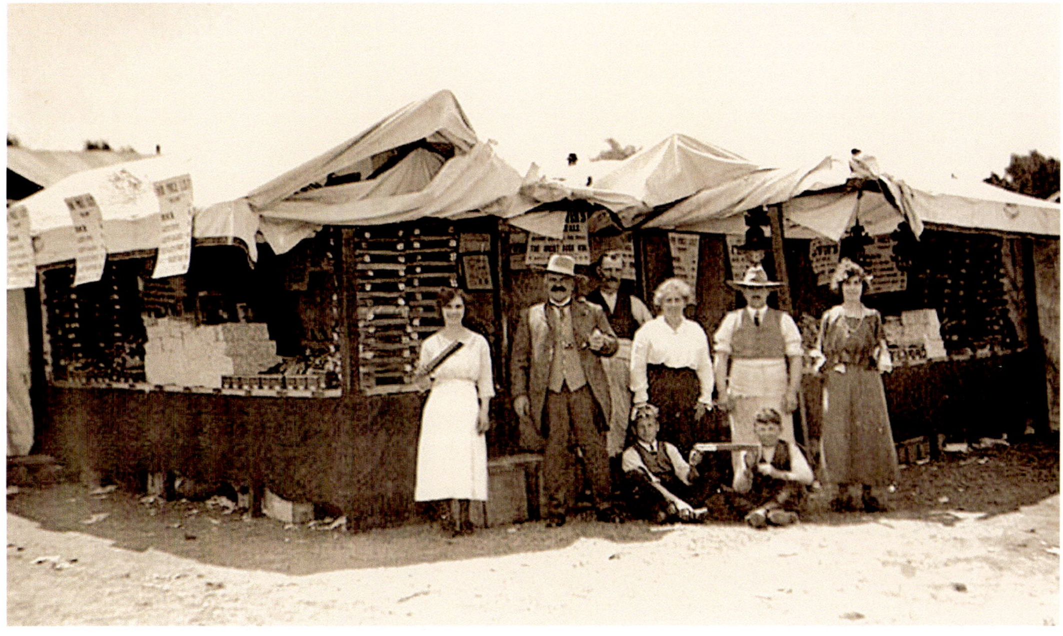

The Paul Pry, Walton

This pub in Walton was named after a nasty character in a play written by John Pool (a friend of Charles Dickens) which was first performed in 1825. The storyline is centred on a comical, idle, mischievous and meddlesome chap consumed with curiosity. Paul is unable to mind his own business, being an interfering busybody who conveniently leaves behind an umbrella everywhere he goes, so he can have an excuse to return and eavesdrop. At the end of the play, Paul Pry becomes a hero after rescuing papers from a well that incriminate more serious troublemakers.

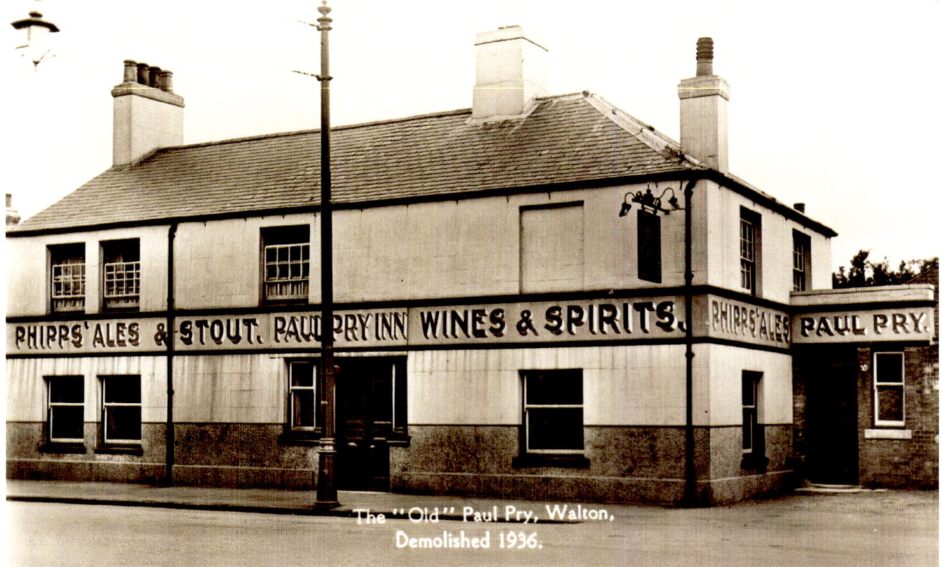

Old Paul Pry, *c*. 1930.

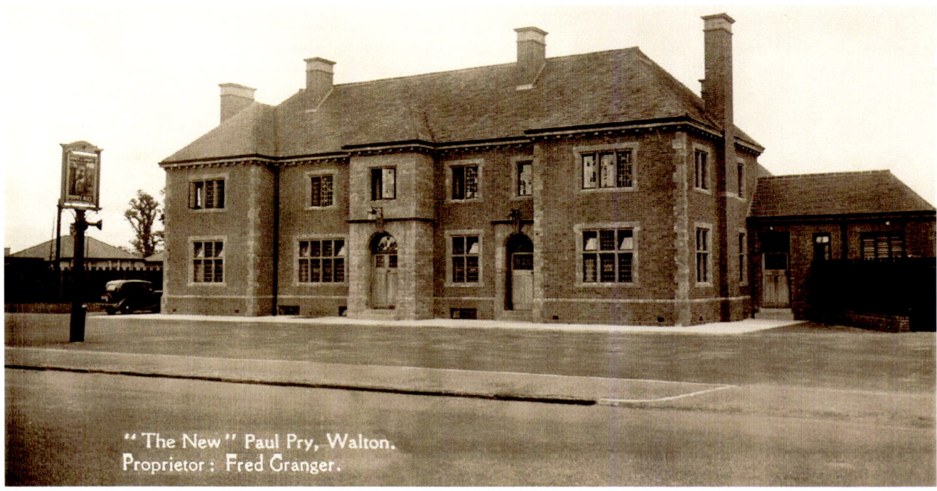

New Paul Pry, *c*. 1938.

The current pub was built in 1936 on the site of the old Walton bowling green. It is a few yards closer to the city than the original Paul Pry pub, built in 1874, which burnt down.

The pub underwent extensive renovation in 2006. On 4 July 2024, the Paul Pry closed down as part of its change of use to a hotel and is no longer serving customers.

Long Causeway Connections to the Railwaymen

The Peterborough Provincial Benefit Building Society in Long Causeway was founded by a group of railwaymen in 1860 who were concerned that good quality housing was becoming hard to find after the arrival of the city's railways.

The bank took over the King's Lynn Building Society in 1967, the Stamford Building Society in 1980 and the Argyle Building Society in 1985 before merging with the Norwich Building Society to become the Norwich and Peterborough Building Society in 1986.

The Norwich and Peterborough Building Society had over forty-five branches across East Anglia. Its former head office was opened by Elizabeth II at Lynch Wood, Peterborough, in 1988 where an important operational base is maintained by Yorkshire Building Society today. In 2017, the parent company, Yorkshire Building Society Group, announced the closure of thirty-one Norwich and Peterborough branches, all current accounts, and the withdrawal of the brand. Remaining Norwich and Peterborough branches were closed on 6 July 2018 and reopened as Yorkshire Building Society branches.

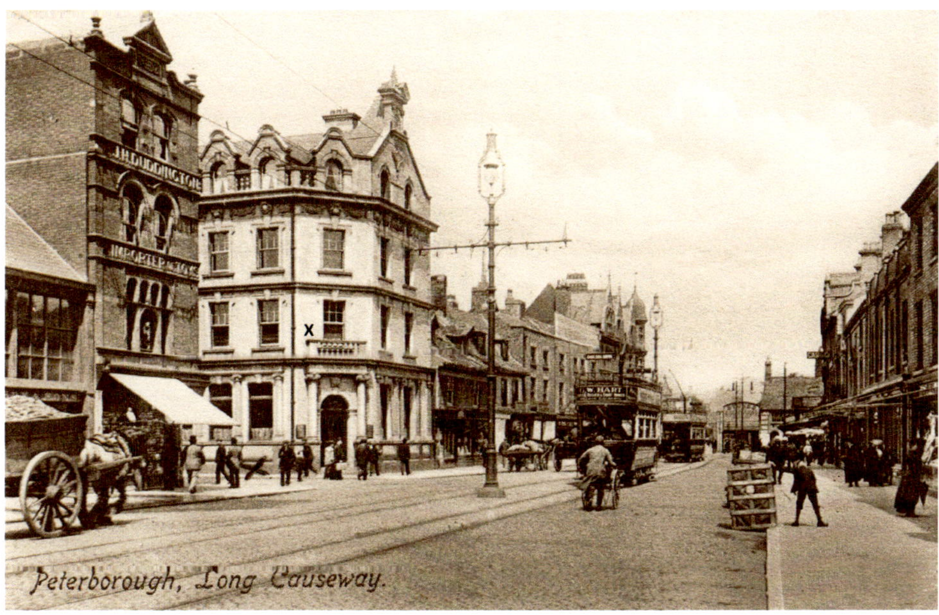

The 'X' marks the Peterborough Provincial Benefit Building Society, *c.* 1910.

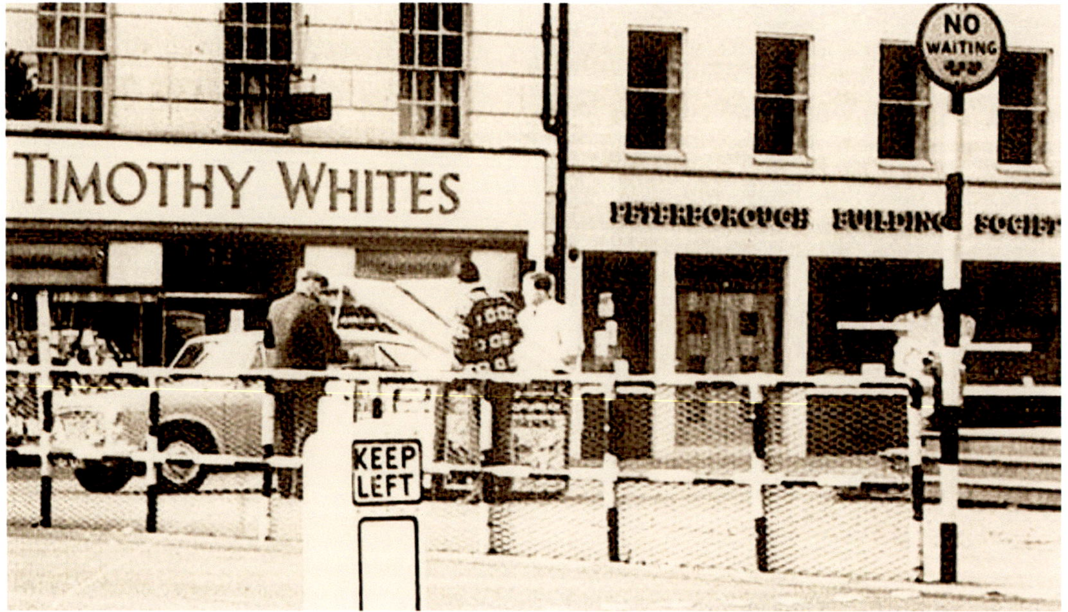

Peterborough Building Society before it merged with Norwich Building Society in the late 1960s.

Election Riots

In nineteenth-century Peterborough, MP election nights were chaotic, marked by clashes between the public and the police rather than political discourse. Crowds traditionally dismantled the hustings platform in Market Square and took the wood, causing shops to close early and board up. Ladies watched the chaos from upper windows. Police warned the public that they could face prosecution for damaging the hustings platform, but it had no effect.

In 1889, tar barrels were ignited and rolled along the streets as people attempted to reach the Angel Hotel on Narrow Bridge Street, which was considered the headquarters of the Conservative Party. Eventually, a flaming barrel was pushed up onto the hotel steps. Efforts were made to bring it through the door, but the landlord organised guests to pour water onto both the barrel and the crowds below. The mob retaliated by throwing wood through the windows. This by-election resulted in a victory for the Liberal candidate, Sir Alpheus Morton.

After the 1895 Peterborough election result was announced, it took thirty-five baton-wielding policemen to restore order when a riot broke out. Six years earlier, angry Liberals armed with burning barrels full of straw and tar had laid siege on the Angel Hotel, where WHSmith stands today, after the Conservative candidate won the election.

In the 1906 election, the victorious candidate, Sir Granville Greenwood MP, was driven to the Liberal Club for speeches and then back to his hotel. Opposition

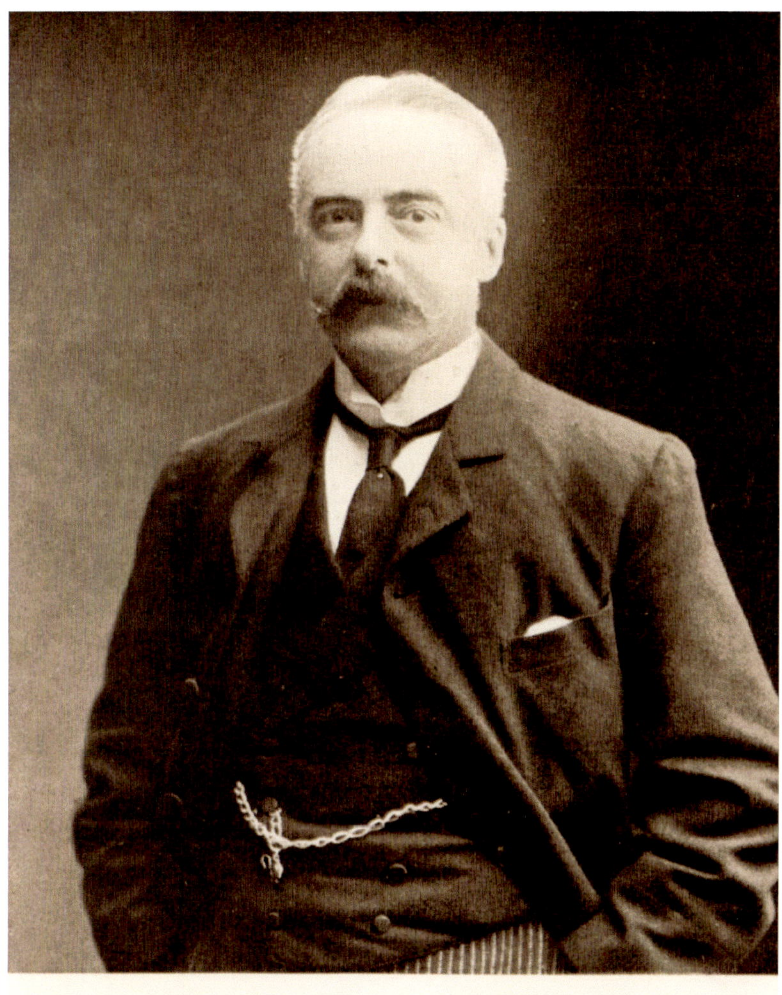

MR. GEORGE G. GREENWOOD.
The Officers of the Peterboro' Liberal Association
send Best Wishes for the New Year.

J. A. HERBERT,   H. B. HARTLEY,   W. THORBURN,
PRESIDENT.   HON. SEC.   AGENT.

George Greenwood, Liberal candidate in 1906.

supports stole his horse-drawn carriage, hauling it to the Grand Hotel, where they filled it with straw and set it on fire. The blaze was so intense that the cab burned completely before they were able to reach their intended target of the Angel Hotel, Conservative HQ.

Known simply as George Greenwood, a writer, he went on to become Peterborough's MP from 1906 to 1918. George was a prominent contributor to the 1916 debate concerning Shakespeare's authorship – some people believe Shakespeare did not write all the plays and poems accredited to him.

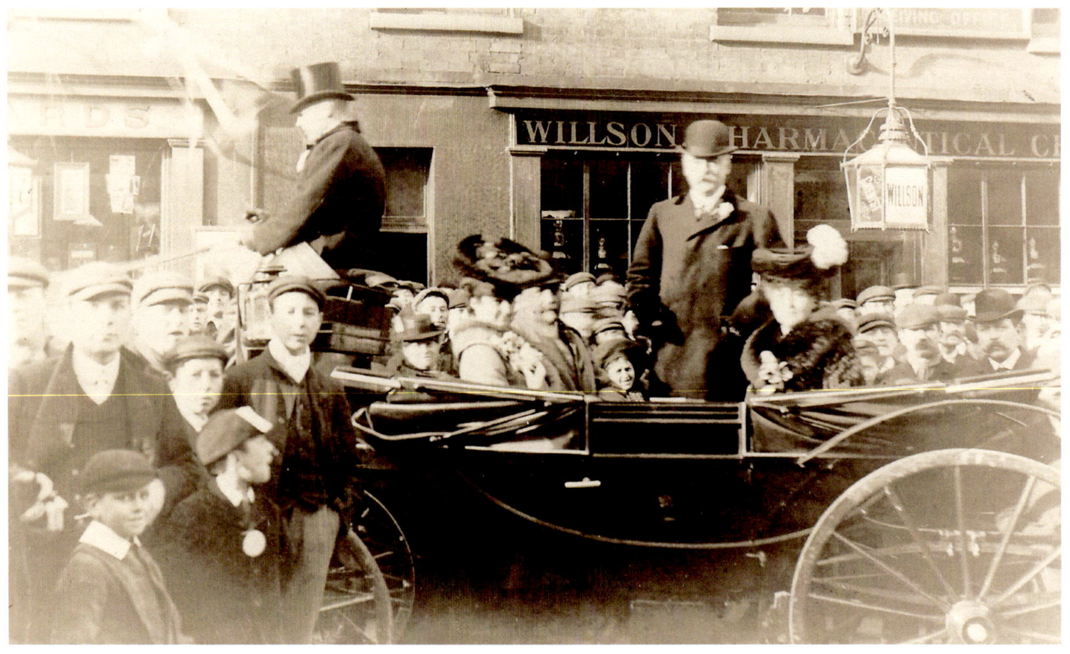

George Greenwood in his horse-drawn cab.

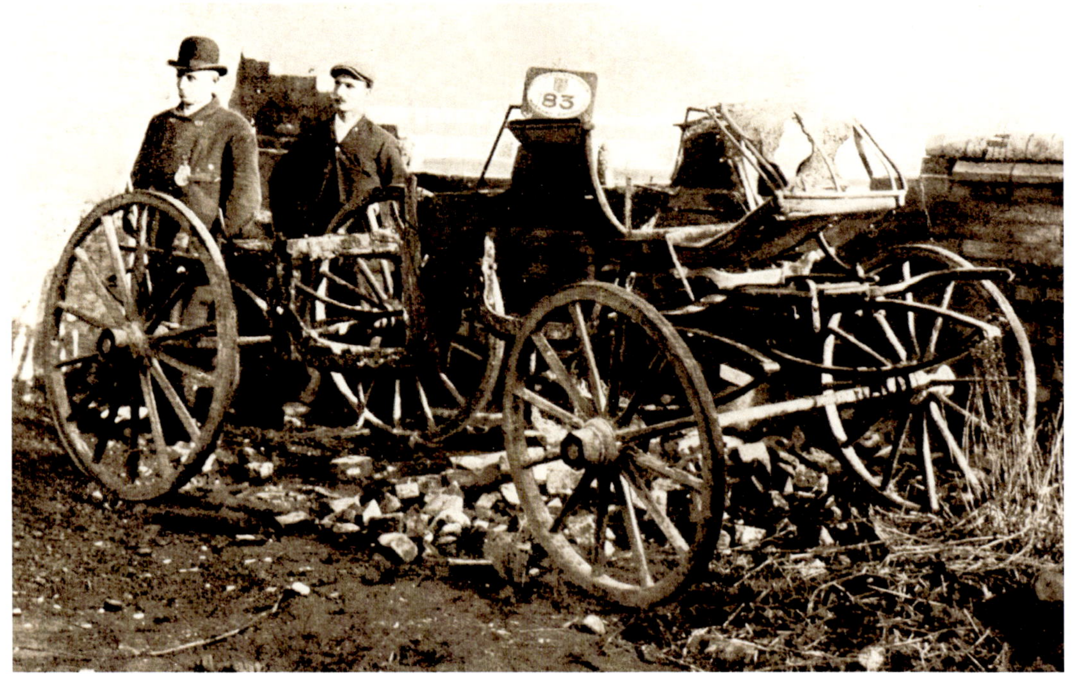

George Greenwood's burnt-out cab in 1906.

Paper Stories

The Peterborough Evening Telegraph (now *The Peterborough Telegraph*) first appeared on 23 May 1949. It was just a two-page supplement inside the *Northamptonshire Evening Telegraph* at the time.

The Peterborough and Huntingdonshire Standard was launched on Saturday 6 July 1872 and cost 1*d*. It changed its name to the *Peterborough Herald and Post* in 1989 but it sadly later closed, with its last issue in December 1992.

The weekly *Peterborough Citizen* was a tabloid newspaper delivered free across the city. Founded in 1900 as *The Citizen*, it was renamed in 1914 but reverted to its original title in 1940, only to take up the *Peterborough Citizen* title again in 1942. In 1946, it absorbed *The Peterborough Advertiser and South Midland Times*, which had been founded in 1863, and changed its name to *The Peterborough Citizen and Advertiser*. In 1989, it became the *Peterborough Citizen* once more. It was published by East Midlands Allied Press Newspapers (part of Johnston Press Group) and was a companion to the *Peterborough Evening Telegraph*.

Today the city only has one printed weekly newspaper, *The Peterborough Telegraph*, which is published on Thursdays.

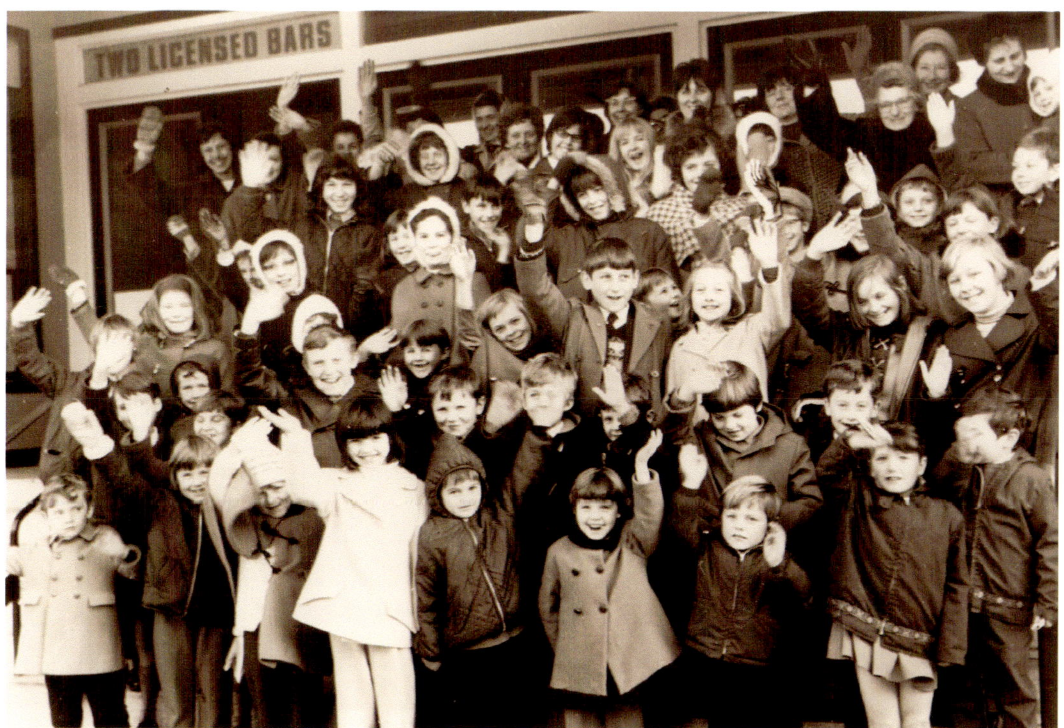

EMAP's children's visit to the pantomime at the Embassy Theatre, *c.* 1960.

Swift Mayors

Maud Swift, Mayor of Peterborough in 1959/60, and Charles Swift (1961/62) are believed to be the only mother and son to have been mayor of the same place in British history. Audrey Chalmers (Maud's daughter) was also mayor in 1980/81.

Charles Swift, who became mayor at the age of thirty, held the unique honour of being the only person to have represented the same ward (North Ward), continuously for sixty-two years, firstly with Labour and then as an independent. He was also Council Leader for almost twenty years. His continuous service of over six decades is thought to be the longest in British history.

Charles was awarded an OBE for service to the public in 1985. He is best known for setting aside fifty council homes in 1972 for Ugandan Asians who were forced to flee under Idi Amin's dictatorship. Some fifty-three years on, there remains a thriving Ugandan community in the city.

Charles was a train driver for forty-eight years and was first elected as a City Councillor at the age of twenty-three on 23 July 1954. Born in Ossett, West Yorkshire, on 2 July 1930, he began his career with the London & North Eastern Railway, starting out as a cleaner and working his way up to become a train driver. He met Elizabeth II five times and drove the royal train twice. He welcomed Princess Diana to the city in 1991.

Over his councillorship, he attended the funerals of 1,700 of his North Ward residents. Charles Swift died on 16 August 2022, aged ninety-two, and was survived by his wife, Brenda, a daughter and four sons.

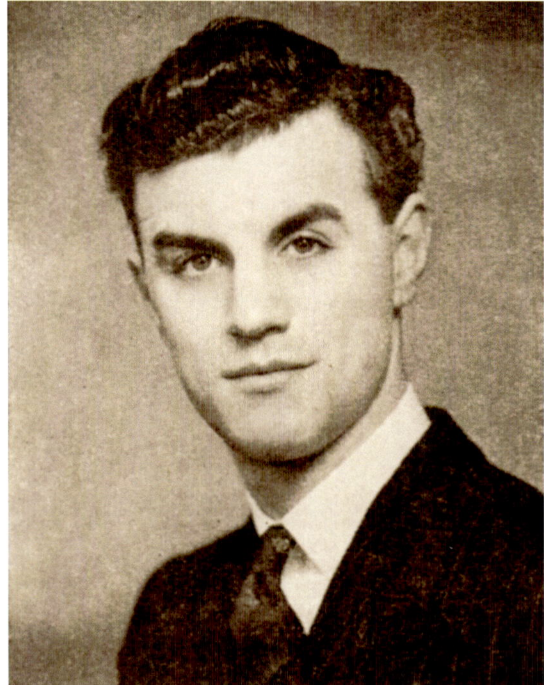

Left: Charles Swift, Labour candidate, *c.* 1938.

Opposite above: Councillor Charles Swift, Mayor of Peterborough from 1961 to 1962.

Opposite below: Charles Swift in retirement.

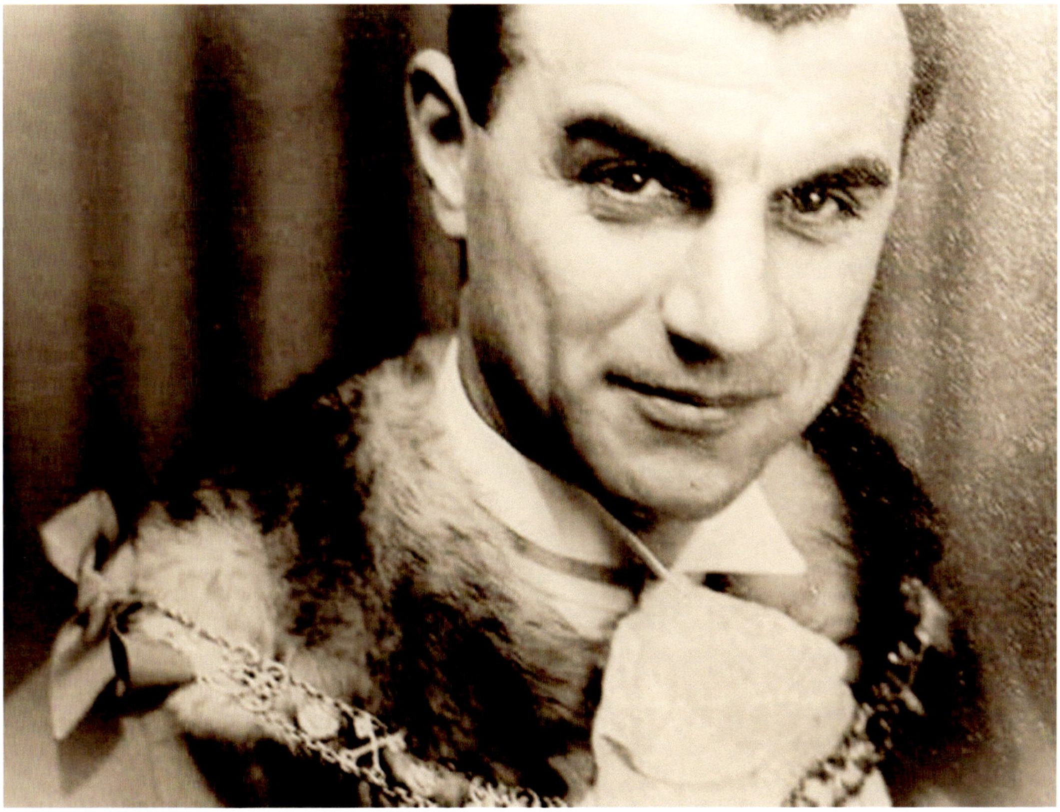

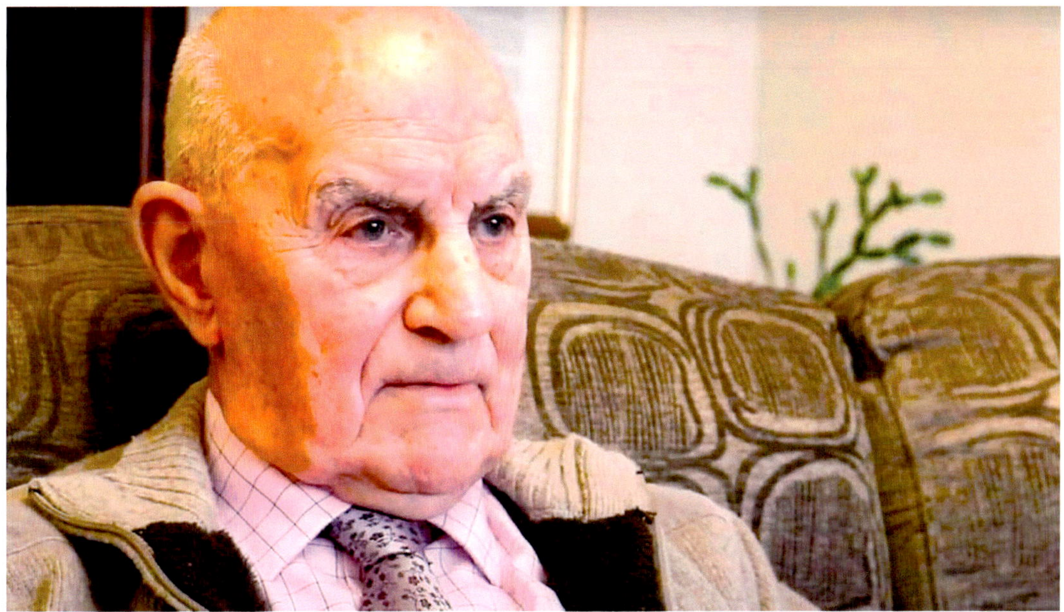

City's First Volunteer Army Unit

Peterborough's first volunteer army unit, the 6th Northamptonshire Rifle Volunteer Corps, was formed on 3 March 1860 in response to the threat of French invasion as revenge for Napoleon's defeat at Waterloo forty-five years earlier. After a name change, a detachment was sent to South Africa in the Boer War.

In 1908, the volunteers were disbanded and replaced by a new Territorial Army unit, 1st Northamptonshire Royal Field Artillery, which was based at the Drill Hall on Queen's Street, Peterborough, and was locally known as the Peterborough Battery. They took part in the Sinai and Palestine campaign during the First World War.

In the Second World War the battery fought in the Malayan campaign and was captured during the fall of Singapore. Fighting lasted from 8 to 15 February 1942. The capture of Singapore resulted in the largest British surrender in its history.

June Bull, one of the authors of this book, recalls her time as a Department of Health and Social Security home visiting officer in Peterborough during the late 1970s. She visited a former Japanese POW who had participated in the Malayan campaign. He was unable to discuss the torture and ill-treatment he and his colleagues experienced. Approximately thirty-six years after the conflict, he still suffered significant physical and psychological effects, and his wife mentioned that he had changed considerably since their marriage.

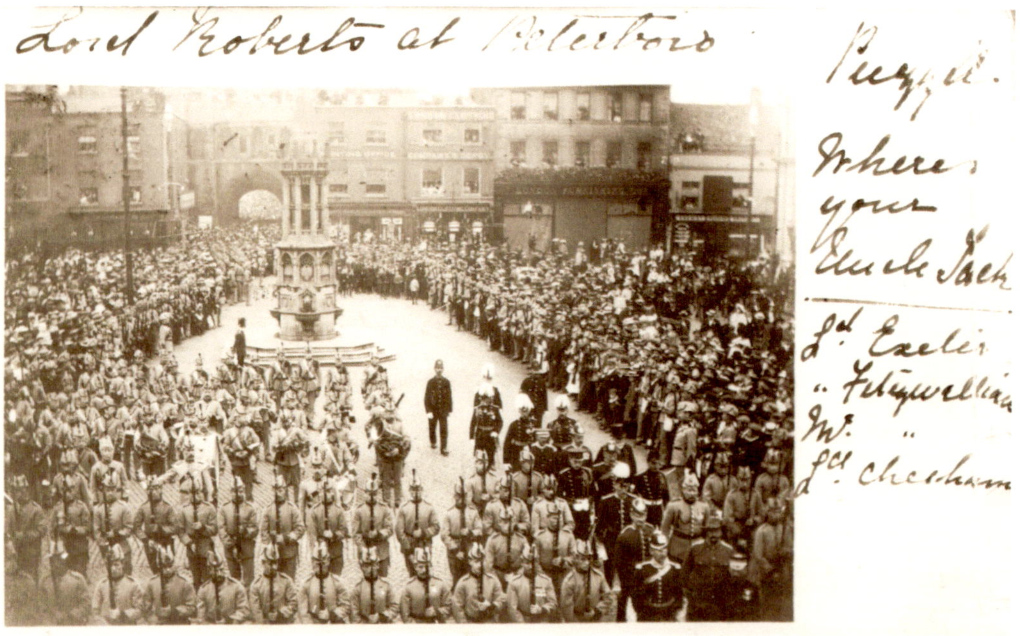

Soldiers on parade in 1903, after the Second Boer War.

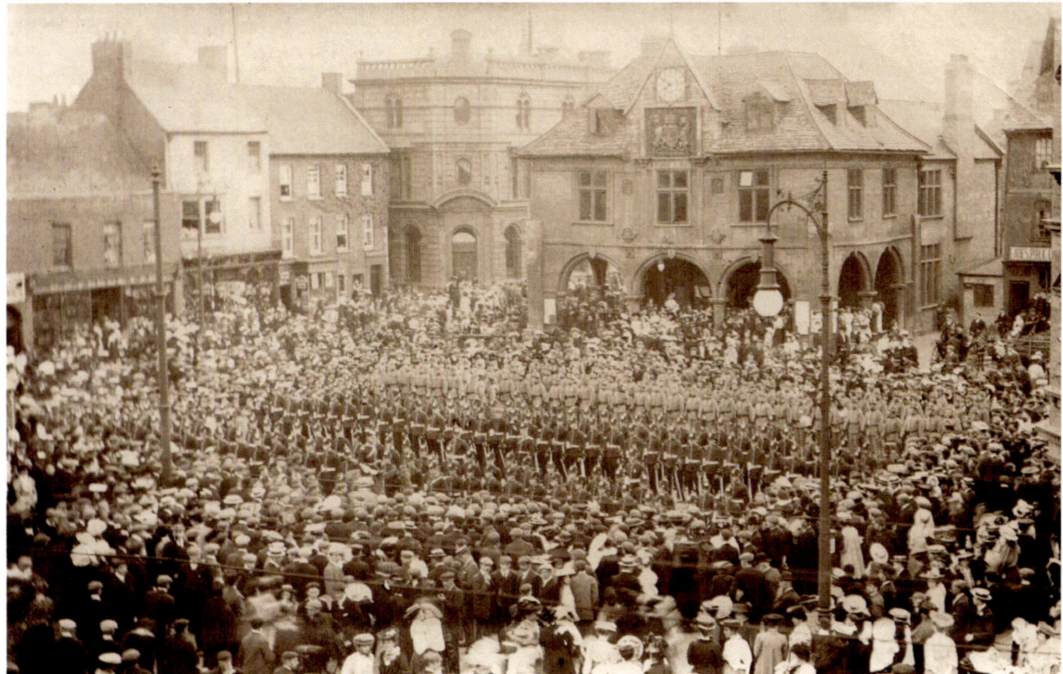

Soldiers parade in Market Place, *c.* 1905.

A City of Pubs and Parsonages

Places to drink, be they hotels, bars, clubs or pubs, have always played a big part in our city's social history.

Following the First World War there was a concerted effort by breweries to make improvements to their licensed establishments. In many cases this meant the complete rebuilding of public houses across the country. As far as the local scene is concerned, the 1930s saw many improvements to people's lives, with better standards of living, paid holidays and the wholesale building of new houses, the latter being assisted by government subsidies for slum clearances. With the attraction of cheap loans, there was an increase in the building of private housing estates.

In Peterborough, new houses sprung up in Paston, Stanground and the eastern part of the city among other areas. Add to this the completion of the Lido, the new Town Bridge and Town Hall in Bridge Street, and Peterborough was a much-improved city. The rebuilding of many local pubs was to add to this new cityscape.

At one time there were nearly forty pubs in the city centre alone: Saracen's Head, Black Swan, The Three Tuns, The Windmill, White Lion, The Vine, The Falcon, Bell and Crown, The Greyhound, Bell & Oak, The Talbot, The George and Dragon, The White Horse, Red Lion, The Still, Volunteers Resort,

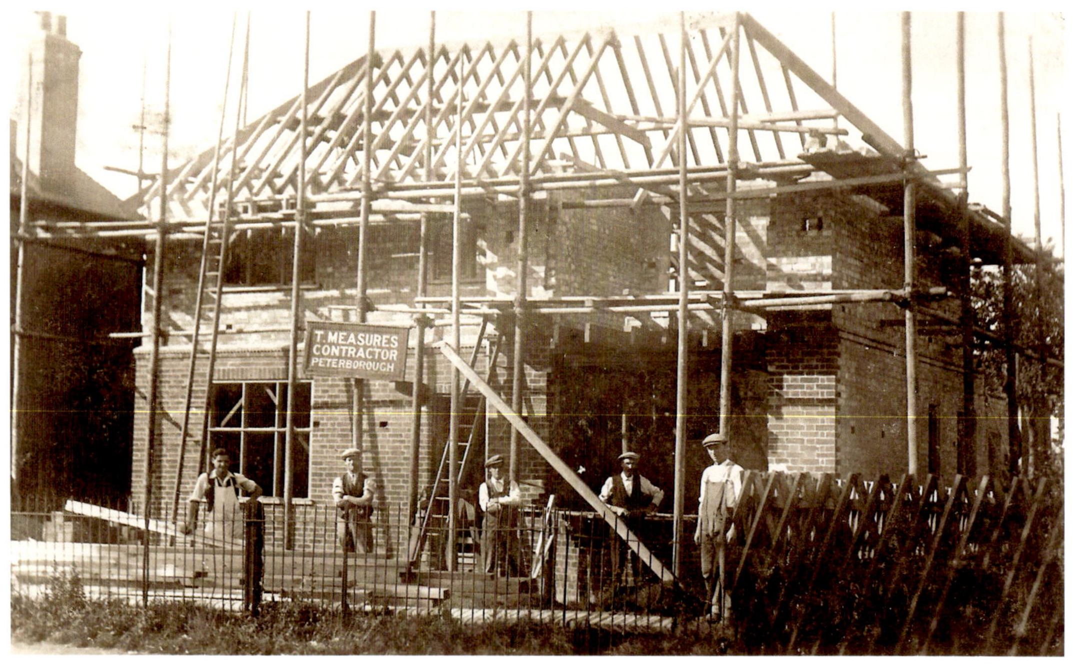

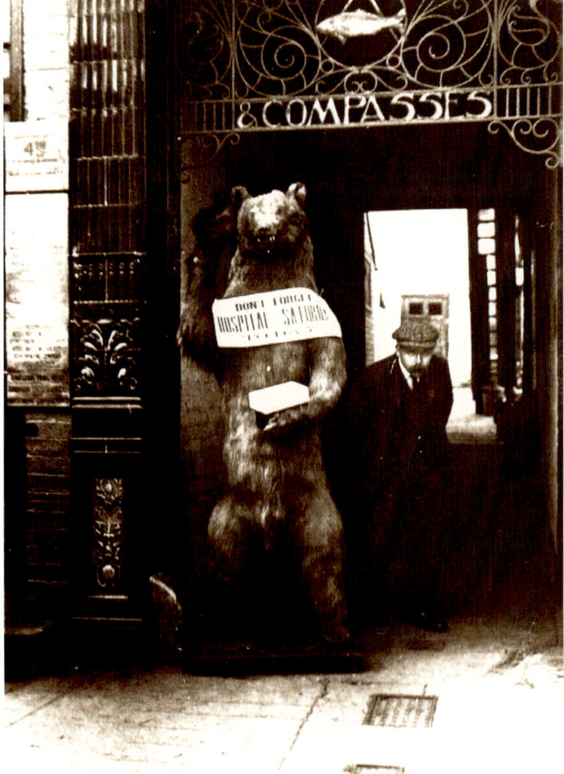

Above: Thomas Measures Building Contractor, *c.* 1927. Ted Sharpe, joiner, is on the left.

Left: Entrance to the Salmon and Compasses pub, *c.* 1929.

The White Hart, Bird in Hand, The Talbot, The Ship, Black Moors Head, Salmon & Compasses, Black Boy & Trumpet, Elephant and Castle, The Boat Inn, Bull & Dolphin, The Bluebell, Cross Keys, The Crown, The Fighting Cocks, Fitzwilliam Arms, The Golden Lion, The King's Head, Pleasure Boat, The Queen's Head, Rose & Crown, Wagon & Horses, The Wheatsheaf and The Wheel.

Not only did we have a plethora of pubs, but there were some twenty-three parsonages, most of which were Church of England vicarages, but they also included ones that were Roman Catholic, Calvinist, Christadelphians Congregational, Baptist, Primitive Methodist, Free Church of England, Salvation Army, the Brethren, United Methodist Free Church and Wesleyan.

It is little wonder therefore that during one of Charles Dickens's visits to our city he noted that Peterborough was a place of pubs and parsonages.

The King of Skiffle

Anthony James Donegan was born in Glasgow in 1931 and raised in England. He came to fame as Lonnie Donegan (singer, songwriter and musician) with hits like 'My Old Man's a Dustman', 'Cumberland Gap' and 'Rock

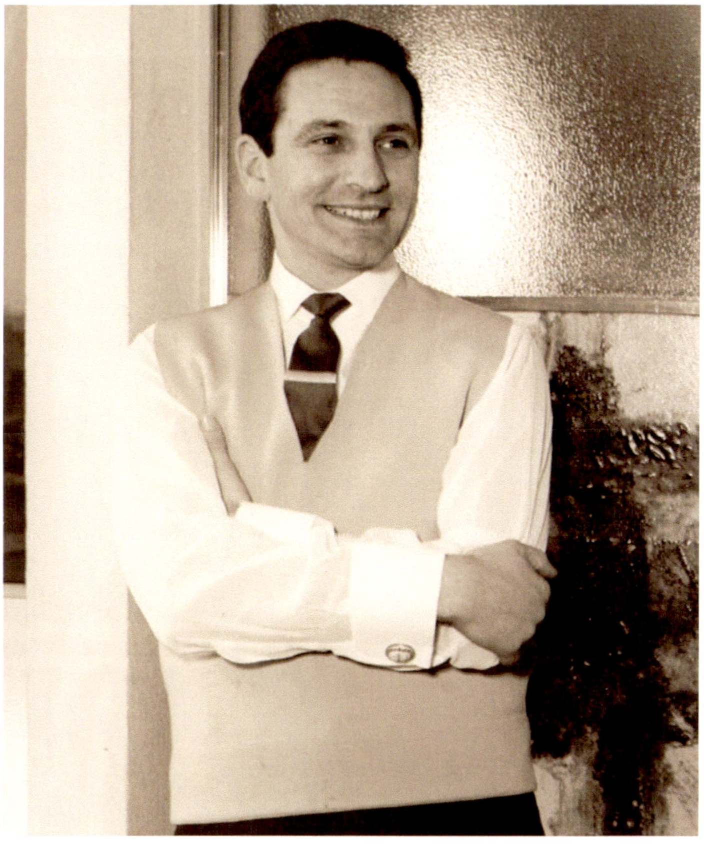

Lonnie Donegan,
the King of Skiffle.

Island Line', but many will be unaware that when he was visiting friends in Market Deeping he collapsed and died on 3 November 2002 at the age of seventy-one. Lonnie was midway through a UK concert tour when he suffered a massive heart attack and died. He had suffered heart problems and heart attacks since the 1970s.

Lonnie was the first British male singer with two USA top ten hits. He had thirty-one top thirty UK hits. His type of music was folk with influences from American folk music, blues, country, bluegrass and jazz, which became known as skiffle.

He wrote Tom Jones's 1969 hit 'I'll Never Fall in Love Again' and toured when his health was good. Lonnie played at the Glastonbury Festival in 1999 and in 2000 was made an MBE.

Before his death he had been living in Malaga, Spain, with his third wife, Sharon, and their three sons, Peter, David and Andrew. He was also survived by four children from two previous marriages.

Lonnie was laid to rest at Peterborough Crematorium and later his ashes were scattered over Lake Tahoe, California.

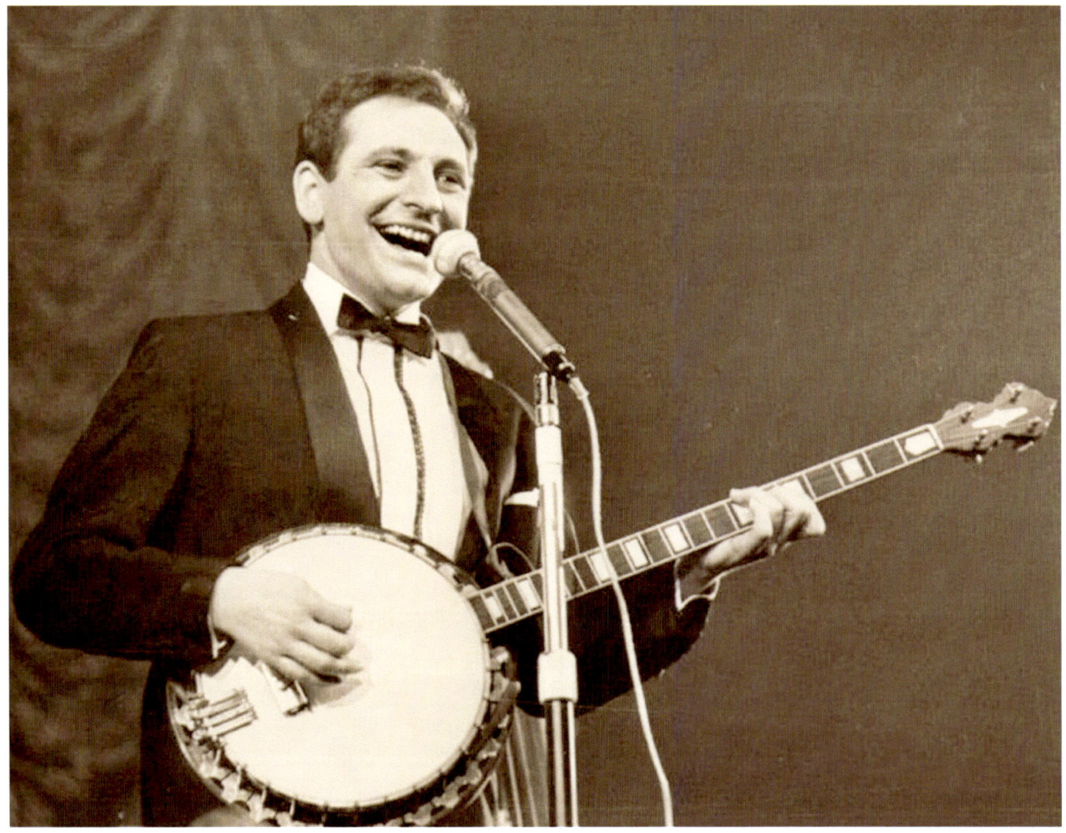

Lonnie Donegan, *c.* 1969.

The Oldest Independent Business to Have Kept the Same Site

The silversmith, watchmaker and jewellery business first started by William Sawyer in 1855 was taken over by J. W. D'Arcy from William's son, Walter, in 1923. The jewellers became synonymous with their landmark shop at No. 7 Westgate. However, as the decades passed, new trends and online shopping took customers away.

Originally a family home in a growing and thriving Victorian Peterborough, the Westgate building with its own rear garden had its ground floor converted into a jewellery shop, with a new frontage added in 1890. For decades, the premises served as both a business and family home for the owners. At its peak, the business generated sufficient income to support four branches of the family.

The business was rocked by the construction of Queensgate Shopping Centre, the financial crash of 2008 and the COVID-19 pandemic. A closing-down sale started in July 2021, with a repair service offered until 31 August.

The D'Arcy family sold the building in 2016 and then leased it back from the owners in Reading with a break clause in 2021. It is then that David D'Arcy, grandson of John William D'Arcy, decided that, with decreased footfall in the city centre and people preferring to shop at Serpentine Green and Brotherhood Retail Park, after 166 years it was time to close. People had started to tighten their belts and there had been a change in trends. David said that people no longer buy

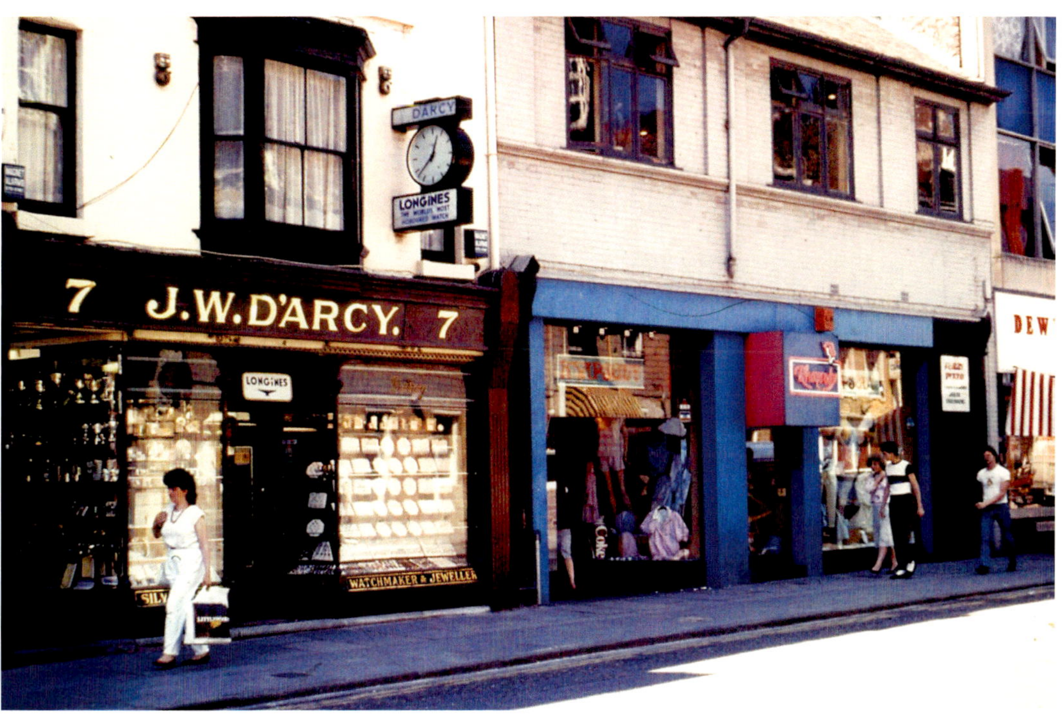

J. W. D'Arcy, *c.* 1978.

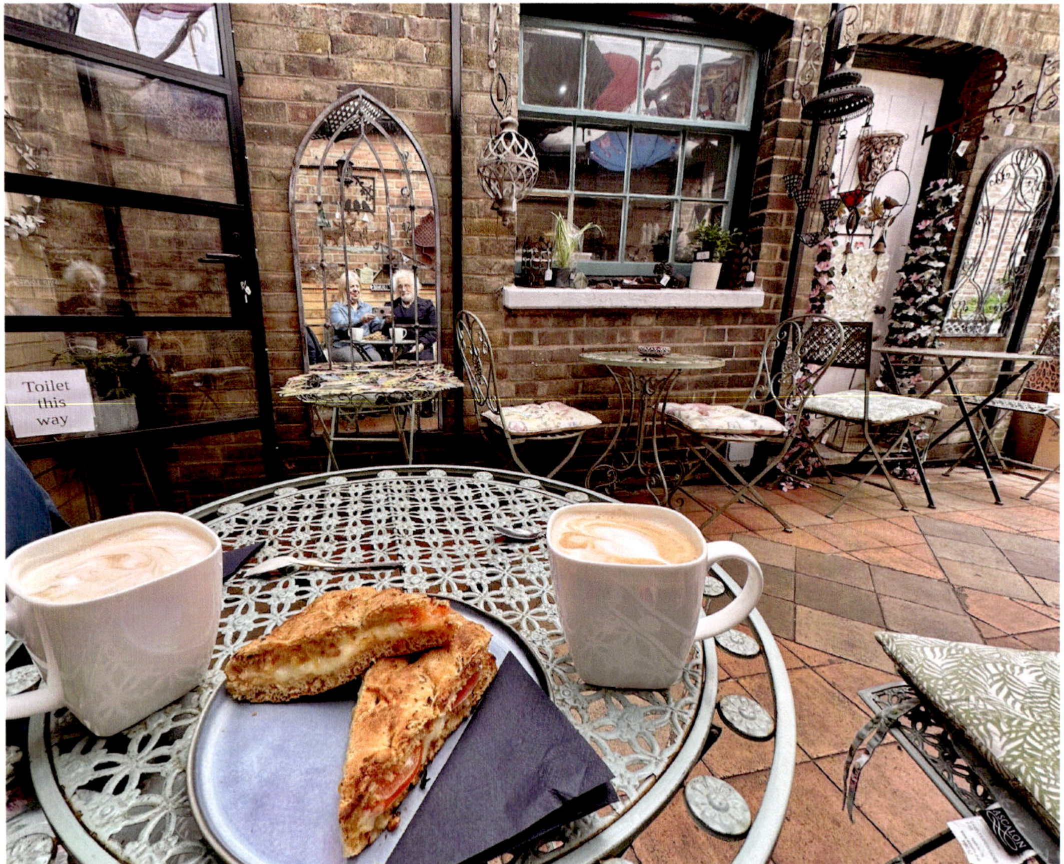

MD Coffee in 2025.

canteens of cutlery and trays and that sales of watches are dying, plus the arrival of Pandora has had a big impact.

The closure of D'Arcy's caused concern about the future of the historic premises, which had its deeds drawn up in 1791. The owners sold the property which has a stone with a carved date of '1678' embedded in the garden wall – thought to have come from the building that previously occupied the site.

Today the business is owned by MD Coffee, a trendy café serving meals and selling bespoke jewellery and crafts.

Bull Running and Other Eighteenth-Century Entertainment

The Georgian period was a time of gracious living for the wealthy in Peterborough. There was cockfighting at the Angel Inn and horse racing on the Common (now Fengate). The town had its very own champion jockey: Francis 'Frank' Buckle (1767–1832), known as 'the Pocket Hercules' (weighing only 3 stone 13 pounds), who lived on his farm at Botolph, Orton Longueville (now the Botolph Arms).

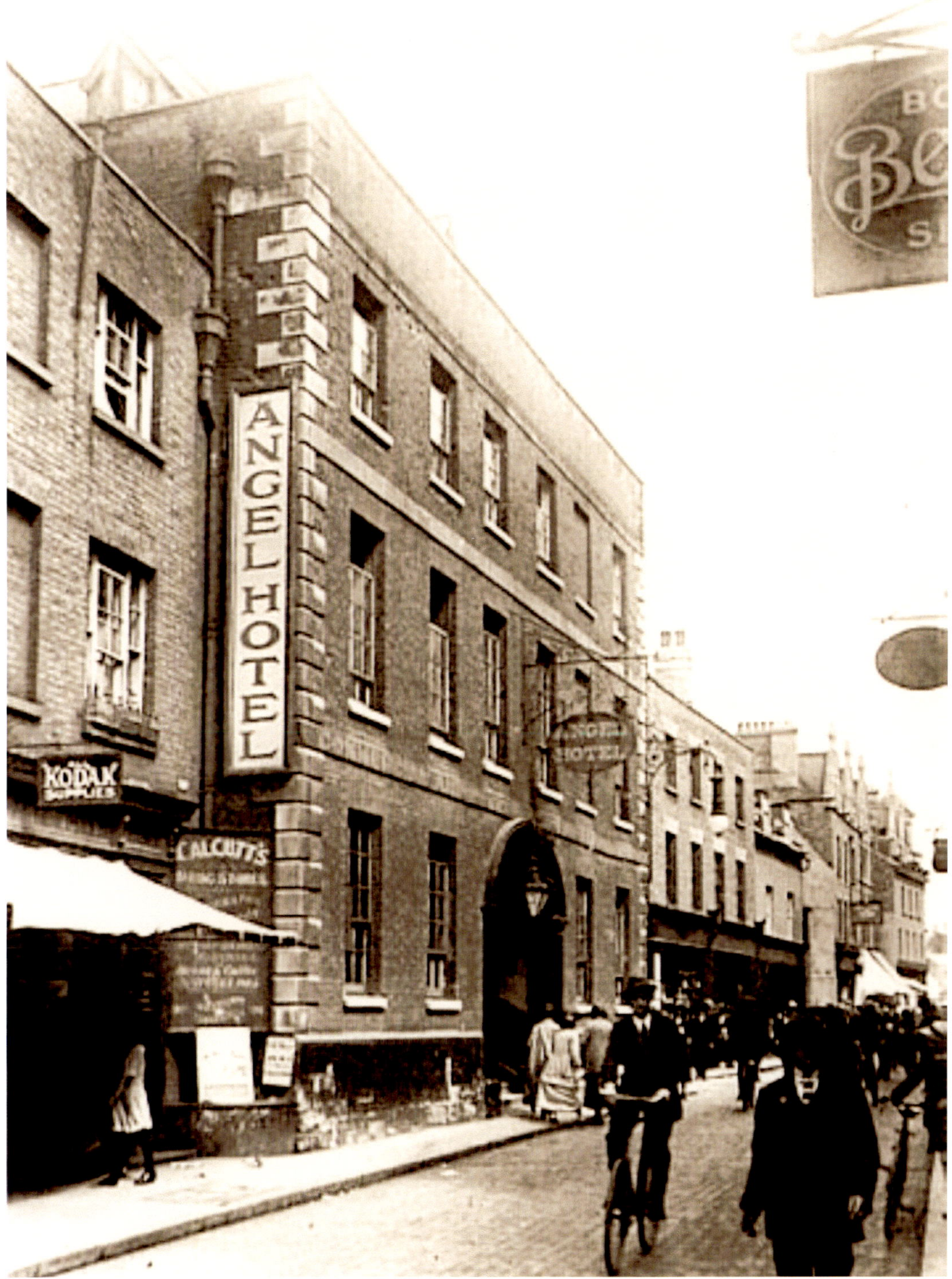

Angel Hotel, *c.* 1922.

Frank's championship record was not beaten until the arrival of Lester Piggott, who won his first race in 1954.

For the less wealthy, the pastime of gambling and drinking plus bull running in the Market Place (now Cathedral Square) was also a well-attended frivolity. Other high jinks included theatre going, where audiences could be rude, noisy and dangerous. Alcohol and food were consumed in large quantities and people arrived and left throughout the performance. Peterborough's first theatre, built in 1774, was sited near what became the Corn Exchange in Church Street, now St John's Square.

D. T. MYERS,

TWO DAYS PREVIOUS TO HIS

EXECUTION,

And left by him with a request that the same might be made public after his Death.

AS I believe that Persons in my unhappy Situation are expected to say something at the Place of Execution, and feeling that I shall not be able to do it, I wish these my Dying Words to be inserted in the Stamford *Papers*, and to be made as public as possible. I confess that I am guilty of the Crime for which I am about to suffer; and for these and all my Sins, I desire to repent before God with a broken and contrite Heart. I forgive from the bottom of my Soul, every one who has wronged me, and I earnestly pray to Almighty God that *my untimely end may be a warning to others, who are walking in the same path.* Oh! may my shameful Death put a stop to that dreadful Crime! *may those who have been Partakers with me in my Crimes be brought to true Repentance! !* I am a miserable Sinner in the sight of God, and I am deservedly degraded in the sight of Man. But I commit my guilty polluted Soul into the hands of my Blessed Saviour, to be pardoned and cleansed by him. And tho' I deserve nothing but Punishment for my Sins, I trust, thro' the merits of my Redeemer, when I leave this wicked and miserable World, to be received into a World of Purity and Peace.

As my Example has led many into Sin, I hope these, my Dying Words, may *lead many to Repentance.*

D. T. Myers.

Signed in Peterborough Gaol, 2d of May, 1813.

IN THE PRESENCE OF

J. S. PRATT, Vicar of Peterborough.
JOHN ATKINSON, Clerk of the Peace.
THOs. ATKINSON, Attorney, Peterborough.

D. T. Myers' execution leaflet, published in 1813.

Other forms of entertainment included executions, which took place on Lincoln Road (junction of Burghley Road, formerly Lincoln Road East) and the Millfield end of Lincoln Road before moving to Fengate. The last execution, by public hanging, was in 1812. These events would have been regarded as a pleasurable day out for the masses.

Hedgehoppers Anonymous and Jimmy Page

In 1965, record producer Jonathan King had written a new protest song ('It's Good News Week') and discovered the band Hedgehoppers (comprised of serving RAF personnel) in rural Cambridgeshire whilst looking for a suitable singer to launch the song with. After King added 'Anonymous' to the group's name, the song was recorded by Mick Tinsley and a group of musicians including guitar ace Jimmy Page, who went on to found Led Zeppelin.

Unfortunately, due to their RAF Wittering commitments, Dasha and Honeybull, who contributed to 'It's Good News Week', were unable to stay with the group and were replaced by Tom Fox and Glenn Martin.

In the 1960s, the band members were stationed at RAF Wittering, home to V-bombers like Vulcans, Victors and Valiants with nuclear capabilities. The term 'hedgehopping' referred to these bombers flying a few hundred feet above the ground to avoid radar and missiles. This inspired the group's name.

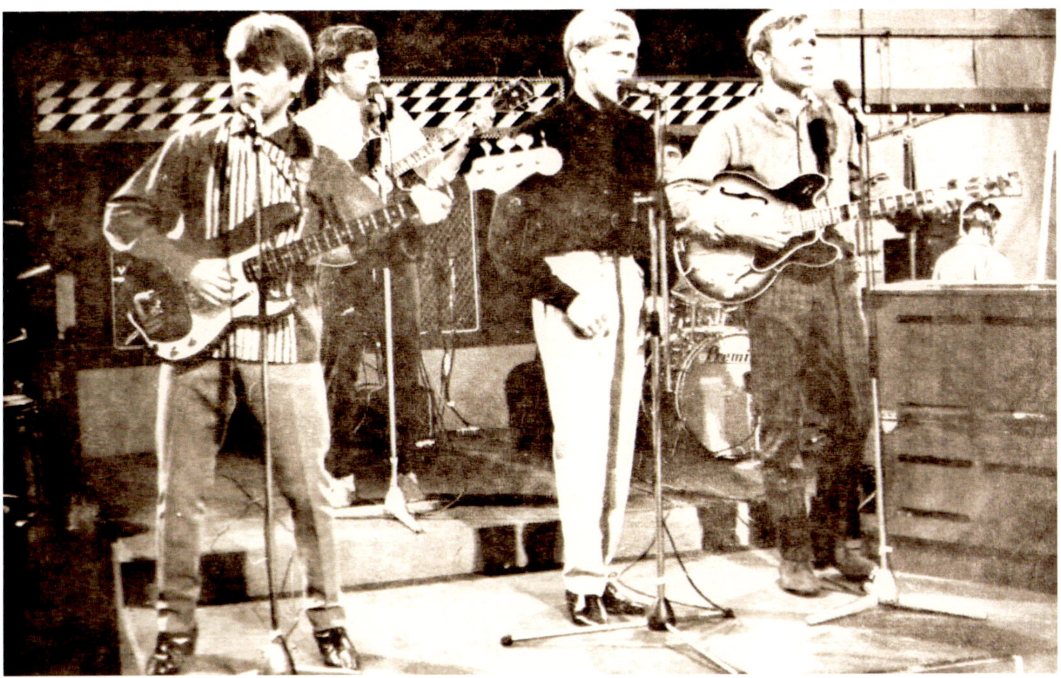

Grasshoppers Anonymous in 1965.

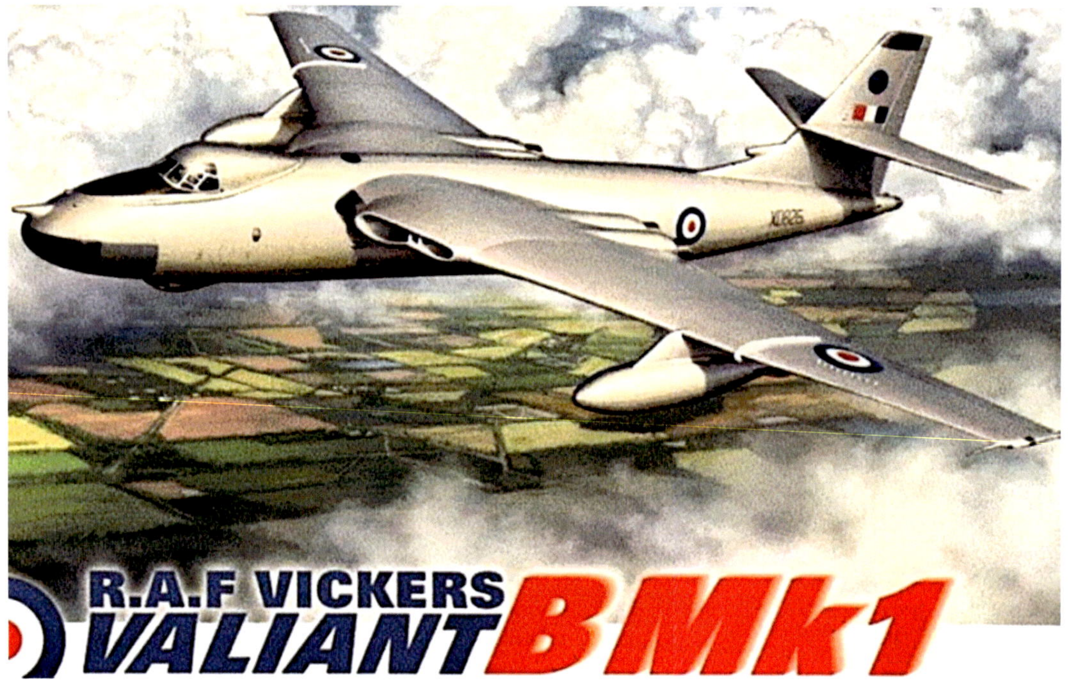

RAF Valiant bomber Mk 1.

'It's Good News Week' by Grasshoppers Anonymous reached No. 5 in the UK singles chart and stayed there for twelve weeks. In the US it reached No. 48 on the Billboard Hot 100. The group released four other singles which all flopped and the lack of further chart activity leaves them labelled as one-hit wonders.

It's interesting that the band and Jimmy Page formed groups with airship/aircraft themes.

King Charles I Held Captive in Peterborough Gaol

In 1646, Peterborough had a royal resident: King Charles I was briefly held prisoner in the city. He was on his way to London to be imprisoned, prior to his execution. He was held in the Abbot's Gaol, which was to the right of the cathedral's west gate.

King Charles had many local supporters, including the Orme family. The Ormes were very influential in seventeenth-century Peterborough, helping to manage civic matters and support the poor and needy. Humphrey Orme was born in 1620 in Peterborough and rose to become the first MP in his family in 1654. His appointment was not a popular one, but was no doubt due to his Royalist persuasions at a time when England was ruled as a Commonwealth under Oliver Cromwell, born in nearby Huntingdon in 1599.

One of the old gaol's wooden doors can be seen in Peterborough Museum.

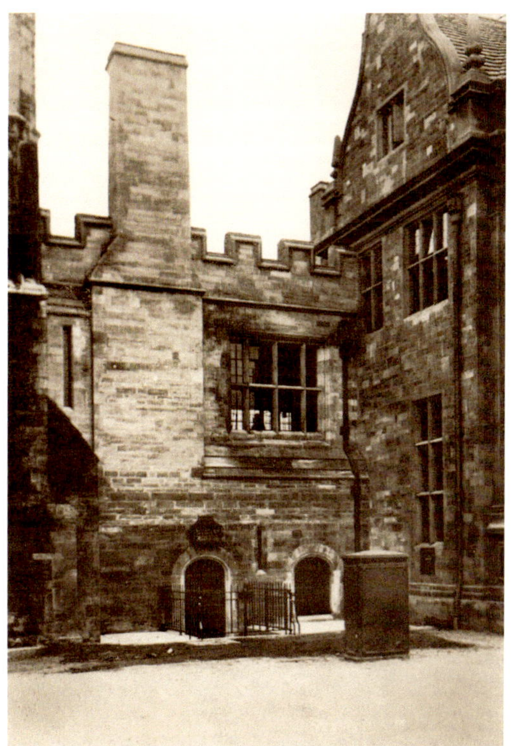

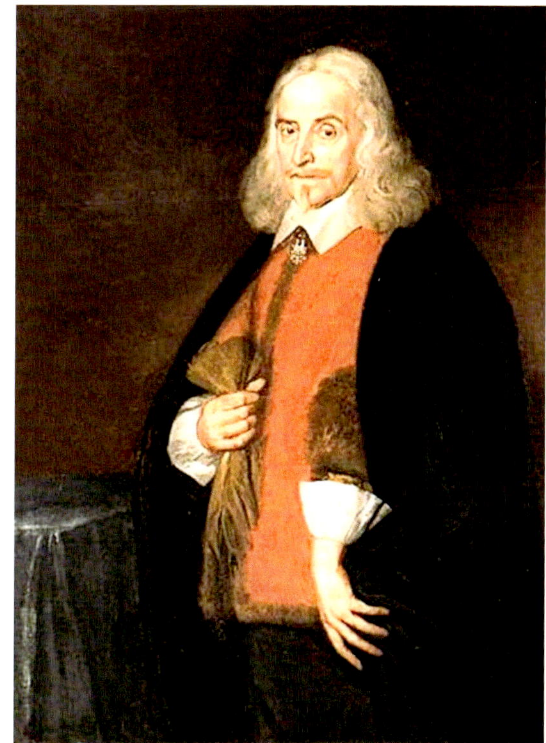

Above left: King's Lodgings *c.* 1930, later used as a gaol.

Above right: Sir Humphrey Orme MP, painting by Jakob Gillig (1636–1701). (With kind permission from Peterborough Museum and Art Gallery)

The Last Sedan Chair in Use

In 1798, the gentlemen of the committee for the management of sedan chairs (a box on poles carried by two men for transport) discovered that many of the sedan chairmen (the men who carried the passengers) had been underpaid. As a result, they issued a tariff of fixed rates. Notification of this tariff was to be in clear view of users. Taking a passenger to and from a dinner or tea visit would be charged at 1*s*. If the passenger was taken to or from an assembly or a ball, the charge would be 1*s* 6*d*. If the sedan chairmen were kept waiting beyond the usual time they were ordered to attend then, after giving notice in waiting, they would be allowed payment at the rate of 6*d* for every half an hour waiting. A proviso advised that the person to be carried must not exceed 20 stone in weight.

Peterborough was one of the last places in the country using sedan chairs. The final sedan chair hired was for Miss Percival in 1864.

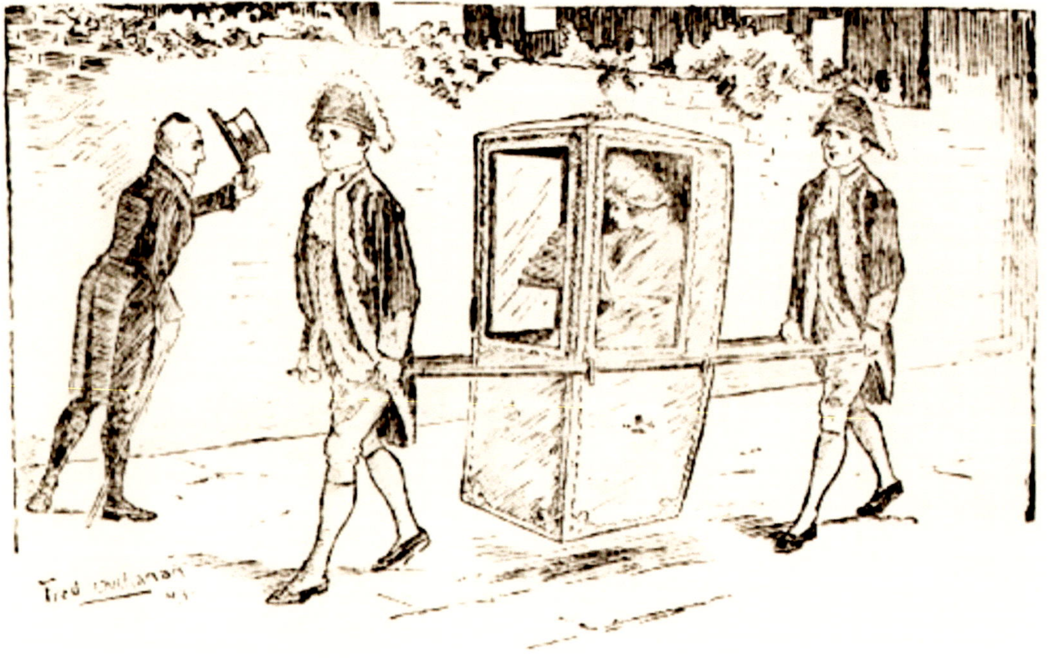

Peterborough was one of the last places that sedan chairs flourished.

The City's First Streetlights

In 1790 an Act of Parliament created a body of men called the Improvement Commissioners, who were responsible for paving, cleaning, and lighting the streets of Peterborough.

From 1795 the streets were lit with oil lamps. Various oils, including whale oil and later colza oil (a non-drying oil obtained from rapeseed), were being used.

As the nineteenth century progressed, some started to consider the use of coal and gas for lighting purposes. The British Gas Light Company was formed in 1824, but discussions between it and Peterborough broke down. However, that didn't stop the city from getting gas lighting.

John Malam had been trained by Matthew Boulton in the creation and use of gas for lighting. His equipment was in use at the Westminster Gas Works, London, when he set up his own private company at the northern end of St John's Street, Peterborough, with the aim of supplying gas lighting to our city's streets. His first gas lamp came into use in City Road in 1830.

By 1844, most of Boongate had gas lamps. Theo Sawyer, an ironmonger in Narrow Bridge Street, took over Malam's business. In 1868, it became the Peterborough Gas Co. with a £10,000 capitalisation.

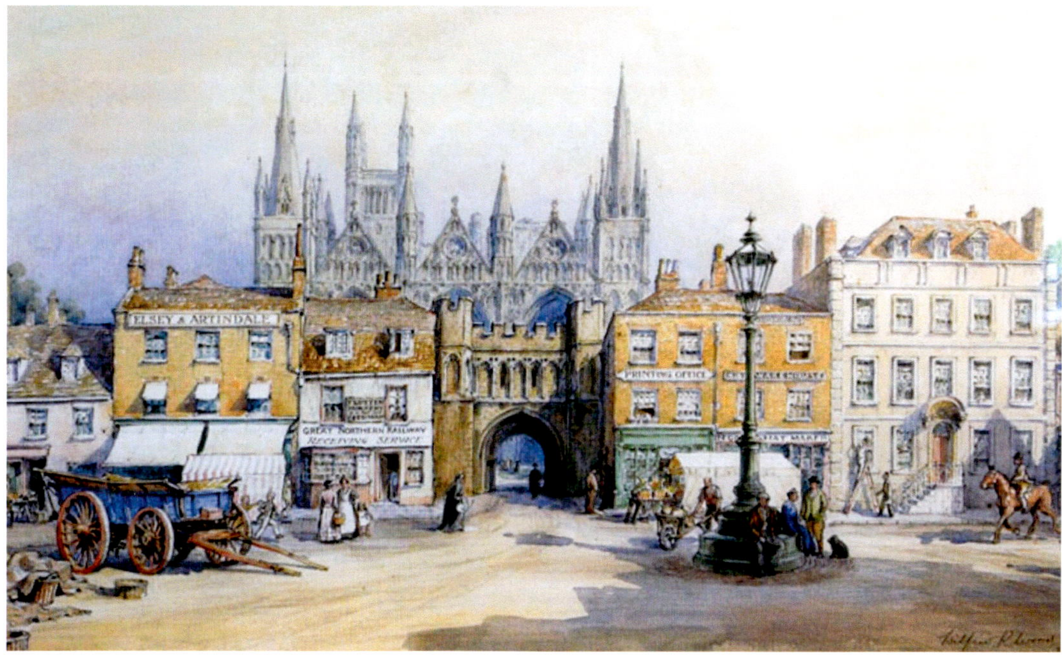

Above: Gas lamp in Market Place, *c.* 1890.

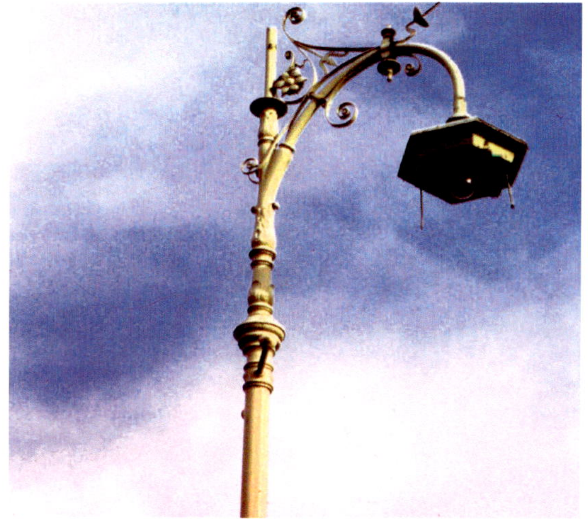

Right: This old gas lamp post by the power station in Albert Place was converted to electricity, *c.* 1965.

The October Fair and a Sausage and Mash Supper

The opening of Bridge Fair is not just about all the fun of the fair but is a significant civic date in the mayor's calendar.

The fair opening is preceded by a parade of the mayor, other civic dignitaries and the public from the Town Hall to the fairground, where the mayor reads the official proclamation. The present-day proclamation dates to 1878 and calls on everybody to behave soberly and civilly to pay their just dues and demands. This is followed by a traditional sausage and mash supper, which raises money for the mayor's charities.

Traditionally, the fair was sited at Fair Meadow, Town Bridge, but in the past it has taken place on the Embankment.

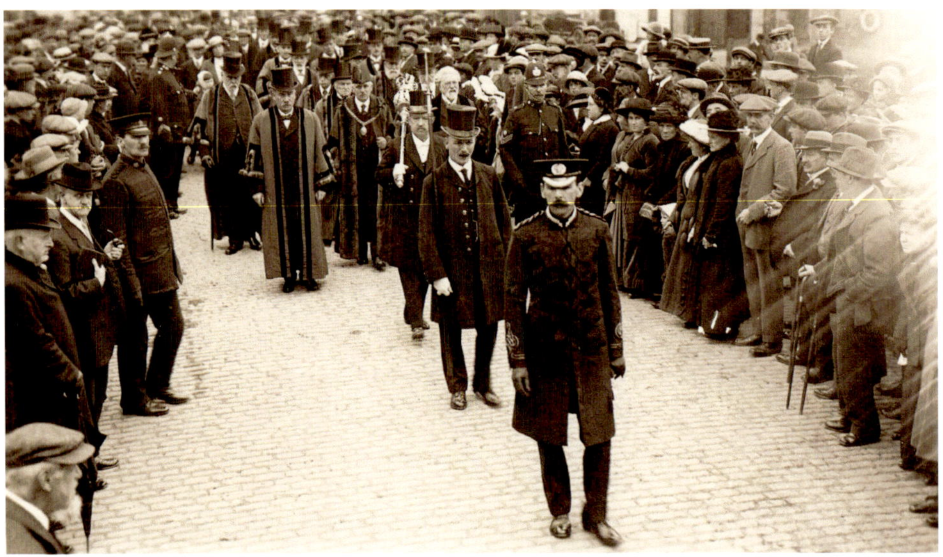

Opening of Bridge Fair, *c.* 1913.

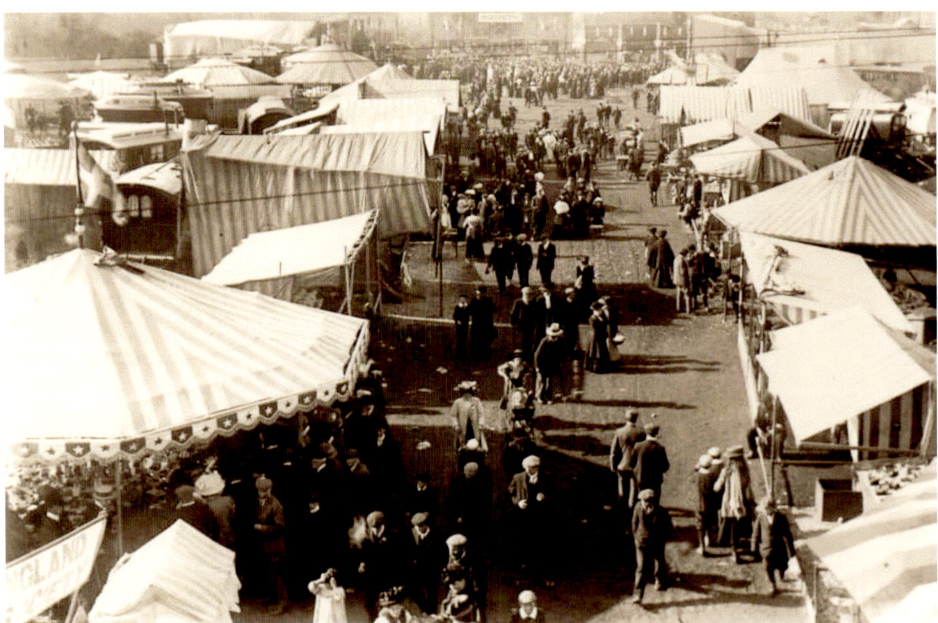

Bridge Fair, *c.* 1909.

Peterborough has been authorised to hold fairs since the twelfth century, including St Peter's Fair, also known as Cherry Fair, St Oswald's Fair and Bridge Fair. The latter attracted attendees from across the country. Each fair had its own set of rules and regulations, and it was possible to get married or resolve disputes there. It is noted that travelling people settled arguments among themselves at Bridge Fair due to its large size, which ensured minimal interference. Instances of drunkenness and fights were reported, and one murder occurred when a body was discovered in the bushes by the river, but no perpetrator was identified.

Charles Dickens's Encounter with a Petrified Bun

Among the famous visitors to our city was Charles Dickens, who came in 1855 and then again four years later. Although Dickens said of our city that it's like the back of beyond, a place of pubs and parsonages, it didn't stop him from lacing Peterborough into some of his stories. For instance, the workhouse where Oliver Twist asked, 'Please Sir, can I have some more?' was said to be based on one in Peterborough – the Wortley Almshouse in Westgate.

Dickens gave a reading at the Corn Exchange on Boxing Day 1855, recreating scenes from *The Pickwick Papers* and *Dombey and Son*. *The Peterborough Advertiser* described the event in glowing terms, paying tribute to Dickens's essentially dramatic genius and writing that our emotions seem to be at the command of a potent magician, who shakes us with laughter or moves us to tears at will.

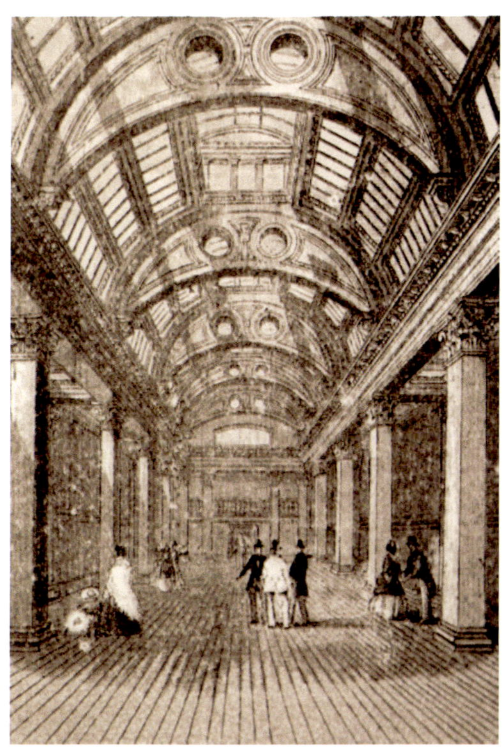

Internal view of the Corn Exchange's West Hall, situated on Cowgate, *c.* 1884.

Dickens seems to have been delighted with the reading, saying in a letter to a friend about the Peterborough event that: 'We had a splendid rush last night; I think the finest I have ever read to.' It was as fine an instance of thorough absorption in a fiction as any of us are likely to see again.

On one of his other visits, he wrote to the dean of the cathedral:

At two or three o'clock in the morning I stopped at Peterborough again and thought of you disconsolately. The lady in the railway station refreshment room was very hard on me, harder even than those fair enslavers usually are. She gave me a cup of tea, as if I were a hyena and she my cruel keeper with a dislike to me. I mingled my tears with it and had a petrified bun of enormous antiquity in miserable meekness.

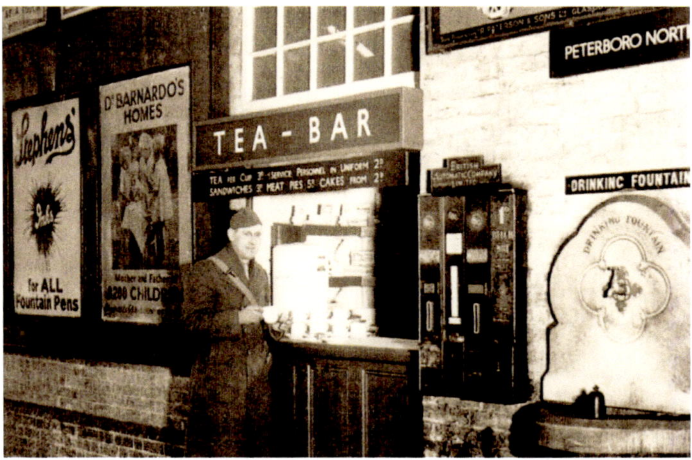

Left: North Station Tea-Bar, *c.* 1940.

Below: Stirling Single No. 776, built in 1884 at the North Station.

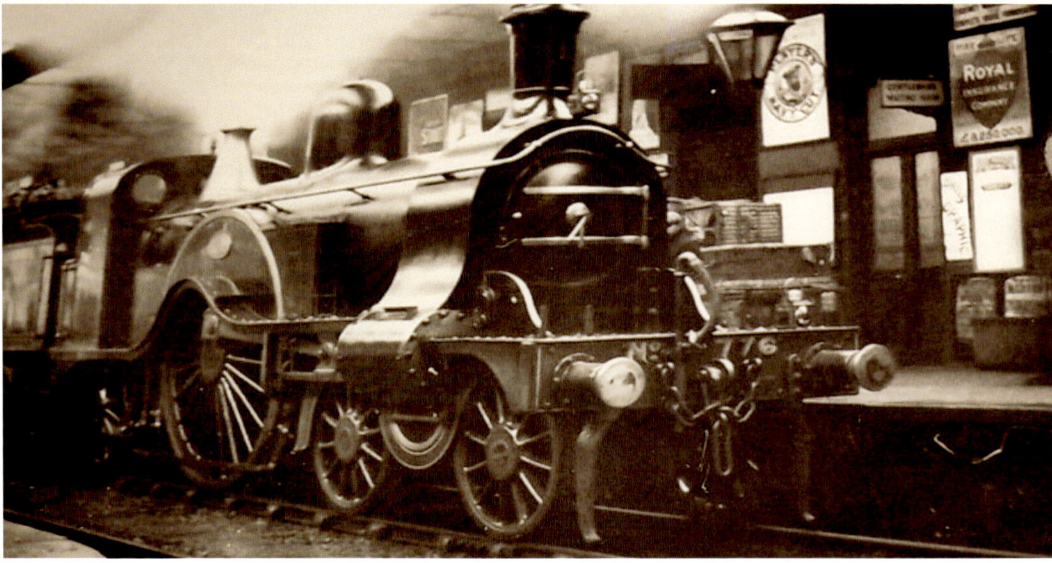

Filming at the Nene Valley Railway

The current Nene Valley Railway is a remnant of the East Anglia to Midlands main line, originally built by the Northampton & Peterborough Railway. This line, which became part of the London & Northwestern Railway, ceased through traffic in 1966.

The last British Rail steam train from Rugby to Peterborough ran in summer 1965, but a few steam-hauled freight trains continued to use the line until the following summer. British Rail steam finished in August 1968, with the last engine in service being based in Lancashire. Several of the last engines were purchased for preservation.

Local clergyman Revd Richard Paten bought one of the last BR steam locomotives that was working in the Manchester area. It arrived in Peterborough in September 1968 and several enthusiasts started to restore the Class 5MT 4-6-0 No. 73050, named *City of Peterborough*.

In the late 1960s, Peterborough was designated a New Town, the only British city to enjoy this privilege. The plan was to double the area's population largely from London's overspill, thus tackling the problem of overcrowding in the capital. Overseeing these ambitious plans was the Peterborough Development Corporation (PDC). One of their desires was to design a large country park to the west of the city. As the Nene Valley Railway happened to run through the middle of it, Peterborough Locomotive Society (PLS) suggested to the council that a steam tourist railway should run through Nene Park's Ferry Meadows, which was enthusiastically agreed.

From 1971, locomotives and rolling stock were assembled in the sidings of British Sugar Corporation, Woodston, alongside the proposed Nene Valley

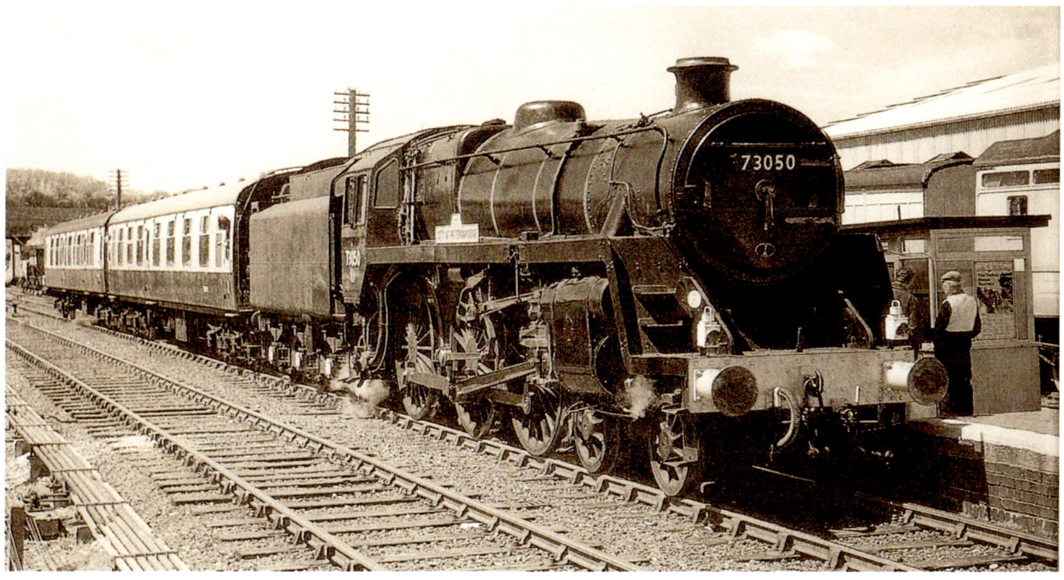

Nene Valley Railway.

Railway. The site was accessed via the Fletton loop, a branch built by GNR from its main line to London Kings Cross. The Fletton loop Nene Valley connection had been closed and removed in 1929. In 1972, the coal trains stopped running to Oundle and the Nene Valley line was closed. PDC bought the line some 5 miles from Woodston to east of Wansford Station.

The reopened line was officially opened on 1 June 1977 after PLS had built its stations, restored enough engines and coaches to operate a service, and had trained volunteer staff to undertake the services reliably and safely.

It was originally planned to have a terminus at or near the former East Station, now part of the Fletton Quays development, but this had to be curtailed due to cost and the eastern terminus was built at Orton Mere, west of Woodston.

Nene Valley Railway has emerged as a premier location for filming anything from TV adverts for chocolate or paint to videos for rock groups like Queen, plus major TV series such as *Secret Army*, *Middlemarch*, *London's Burning* and *Casualty*. The most ambitious projects included the filming of James Bond's *Octopussy* and *Goldeneye*. The latter featured plenty of action, including a scene where a helicopter takes off from a train.

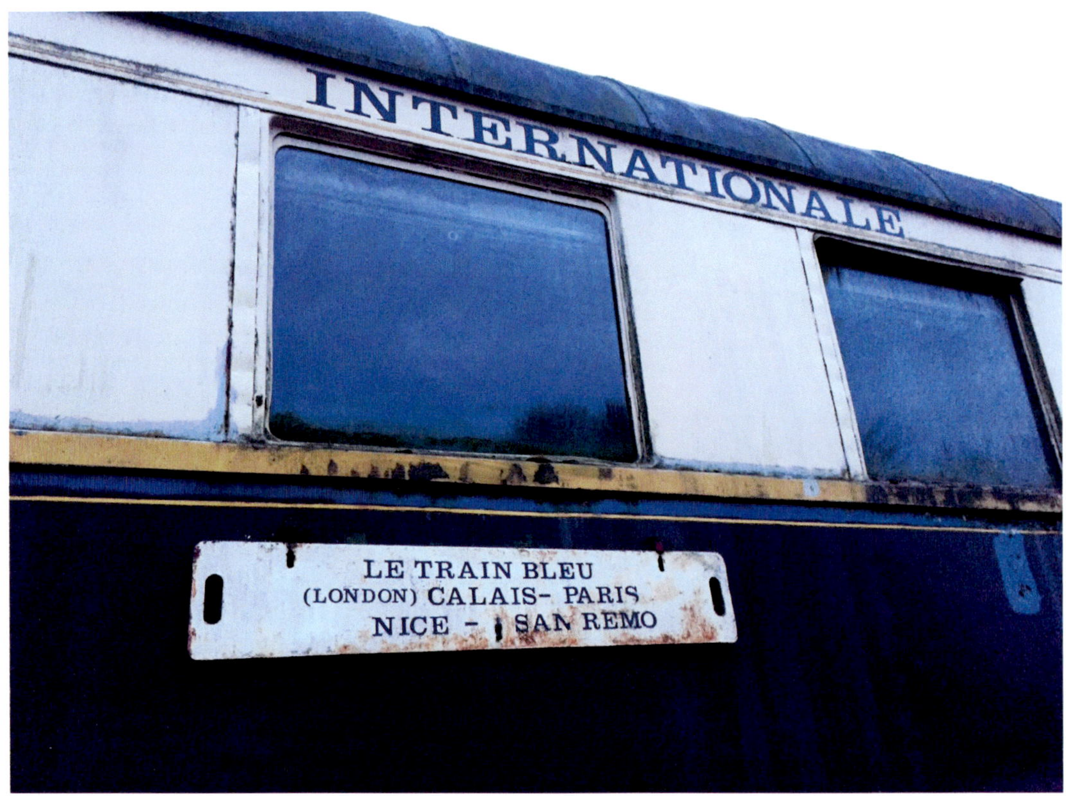

Nene Valley Railway's 'Blue Train' carriage.

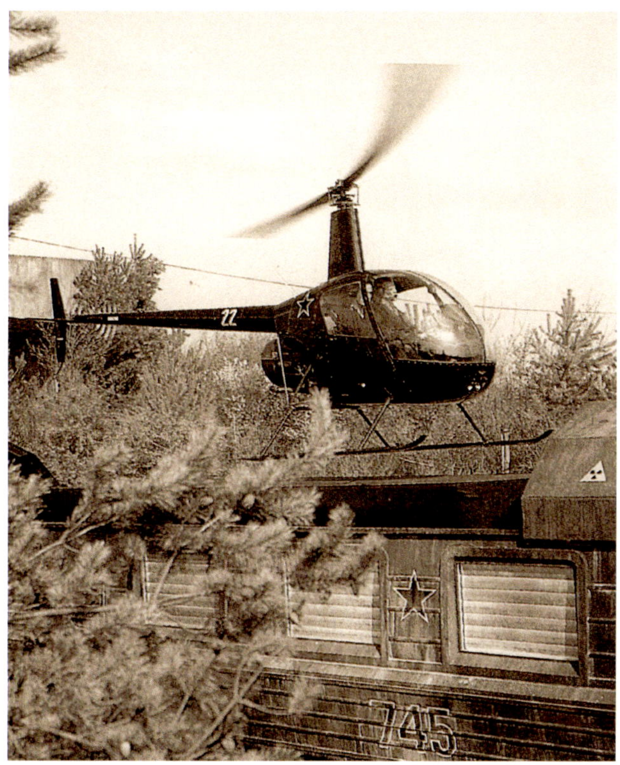

Filming of *Goldeneye* at the Nene Valley Railway in 1995.

John Landen, Mathematical Genius

John Landen was born in Peakirk on 23 January 1719 and died at Milton Ferry on 15 January 1790, just prior to his seventy-first birthday. He was the eldest of three sons born to Elizabeth (née Cole) and her husband, Matthew.

John, a trained surveyor, worked on the Fen drainage before serving as land agent for Thomas Wentworth, Earl Fitzwilliam of Milton Hall, from 1762 to 1788. Despite his career, his true passion was mathematics. He was admired by his peers as a genius, but he had a difficult temperament, often using foul language. He lived reclusively with his wife, Elizabeth, and their two daughters, first in Walton, Peterborough, from 1740 to 1762, and then on Earl Fitzwilliam's estate at Milton Ferry.

His disgraceful language is evidenced in his arguments with such eminent people as the Swiss mathematical genius Leonhard Euler and Scottish genius Matthew Stewart. That said, it's recorded in *The Gentlemen's Magazine* that he had great integrity, strict humanity and a readiness to serve everyone to the utmost of his power and that he enjoyed the respect and esteem from all who knew him.

He was called the English d'Alembert and in 1766 was elected as a fellow of the Royal Society London in recognition of his research and work on elliptic integrals, calculus and rotary motion. He also was a keen astronomer and enjoyed physics.

THE

Refidual Analyfis;

A

NEW BRANCH

OF THE

ALGEBRAIC ART,

Of very extenfive Use, both in Pure Mathematics,
and Natural Philofophy.

BOOK I.

By JOHN LANDEN.

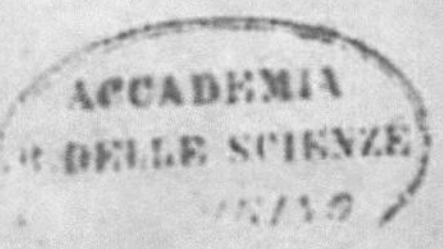

LONDON,

Printed for the AUTHOR; and fold by L. HAWES, W. CLARKE,
and R. COLLINS, at the *Red Lion* in *Pater-nofter Row*.

MDCCLXIV.

John Landen's book *Residual Analysis* was published in 1764.

Landen wrote and published a two-volume set called *Mathematical Memoirs* (1780–89) which contains what is now known as Landen's theorem. He also tried to simplify calculus by applying it to geometry and algebra.

His mathematical genius extended to solving the problem of the spinning top, and he explained Issac Newton's error in calculating its precision. Landen also corrected Matthew Stewart's result on the distance of the sun from the Earth in 1771.

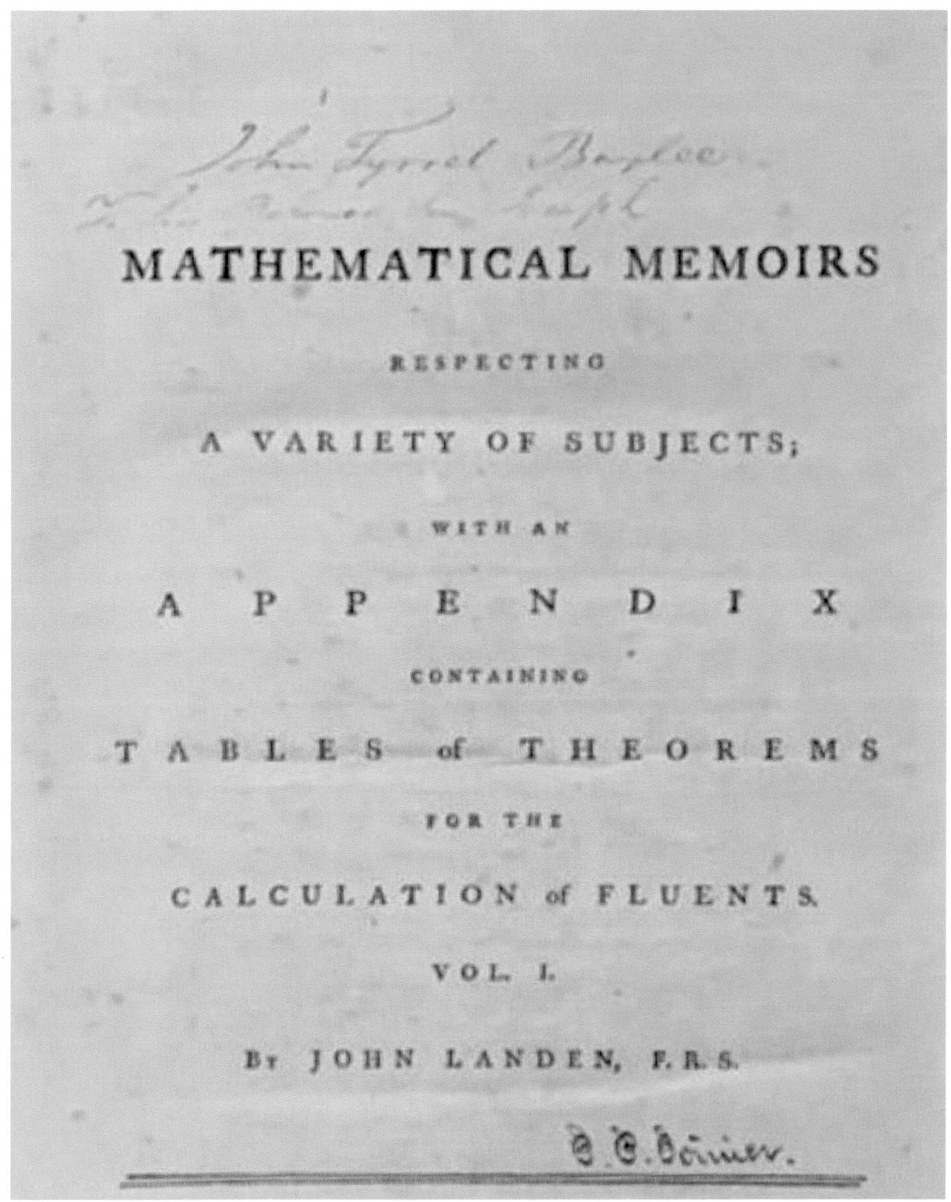

John Landen's *Mathematical Memoirs* was published in 1780.

Bridge Street Pubs

It was Charles Dickens who remarked on his visit in 1855 that Peterborough is a place of parsonages and pubs. Indeed, Broad Bridge Street and Narrow Bridge Street boasted ten in 1892: The Boat Inn, No. 58 Broad Bridge Street; The Bull and Dolphin, No. 94 Broad Bridge Street; King's Head, Broad Bridge

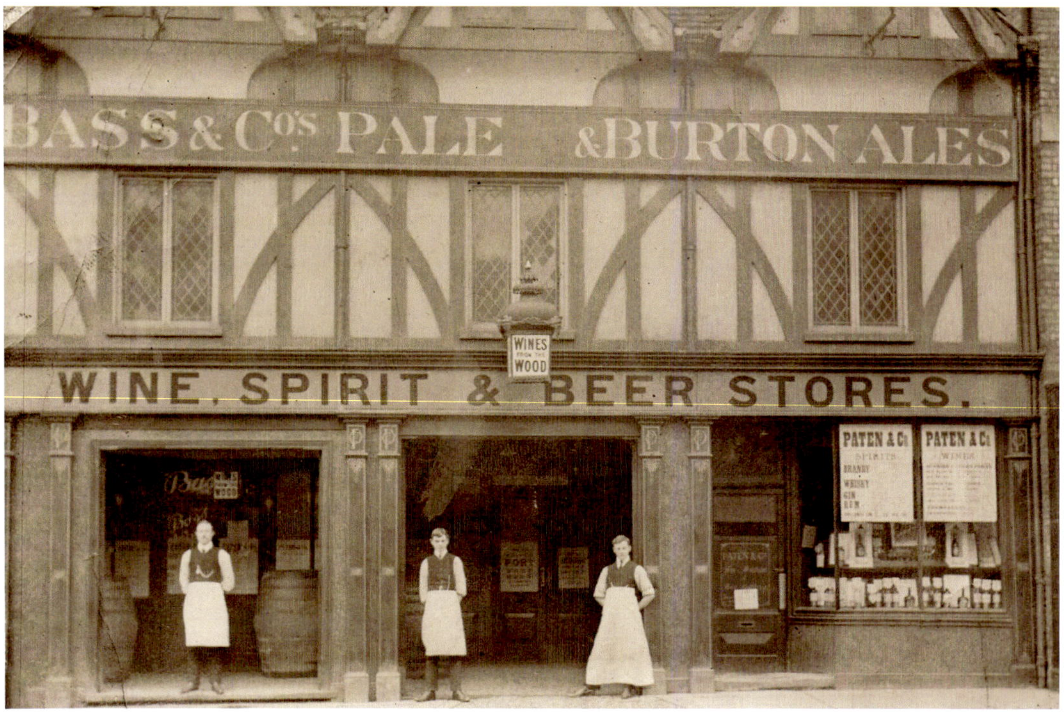

Bull & Dolphin pub, *c.* 1909.

Street; Queen's Head, Broad Bridge Street; Rose and Crown, No. 114 Broad Bridge Street; Royal Arms, Broad Bridge Street; Spread Eagle, No. 26 Broad Bridge Street; the Black Swan, Nos 37–38 Narrow Bridge Street; Wagon and Horses, No. 32 Narrow Bridge Street; and The Fig Tree, Narrow Bridge Street.

Victorian pubs proliferated as urban areas grew with abundant jobs and railway connectivity. They established class distinctions, offering first-, second- and third-class services. These pubs featured multiple rooms and bars to serve various classes and customers, becoming a significant part of British culture during the Victorian era.

Pubs were community hubs, offering alcoholic drinks, games and conversations that influenced local politics and society. They often hosted meetings for political groups and trade unions.

Victorian pubs hosted public lectures and debates, making them key intellectual hubs. They also provided a social refuge from harsh urban life.

Today, everyone and anyone is welcome in the great British pub. So welcome, in fact, that almost one in four Britons meet their future husband or wife in a pub. Currently, there are no traditional pubs remaining on Bridge Street; instead, the area is populated with eateries and restaurants that also serve alcohol.

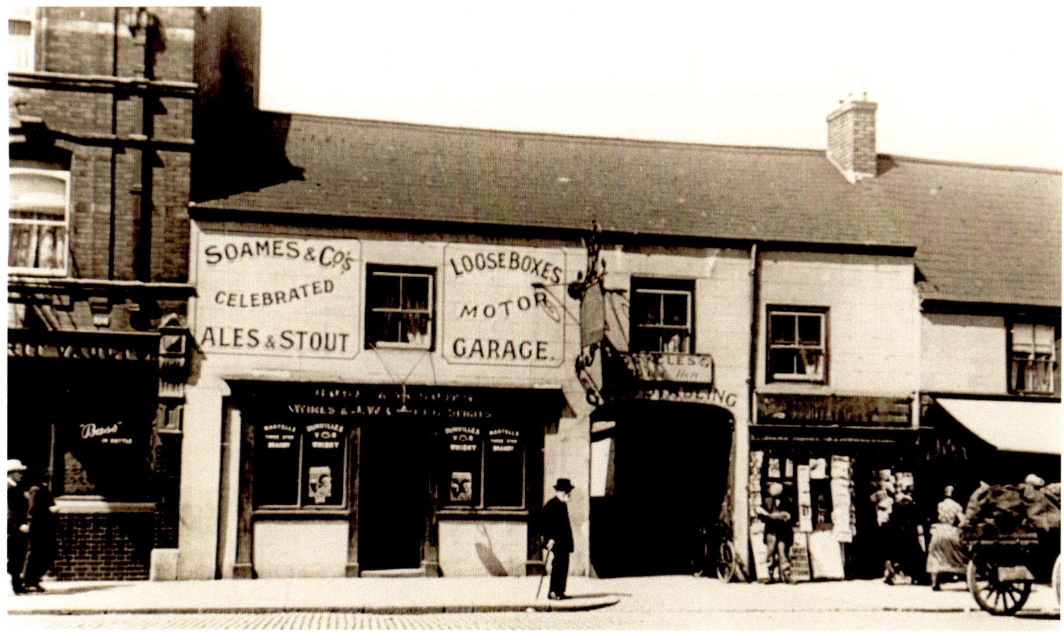

The Rose & Crown pub is to the centre with the Boat Inn on the left, *c.* 1912.

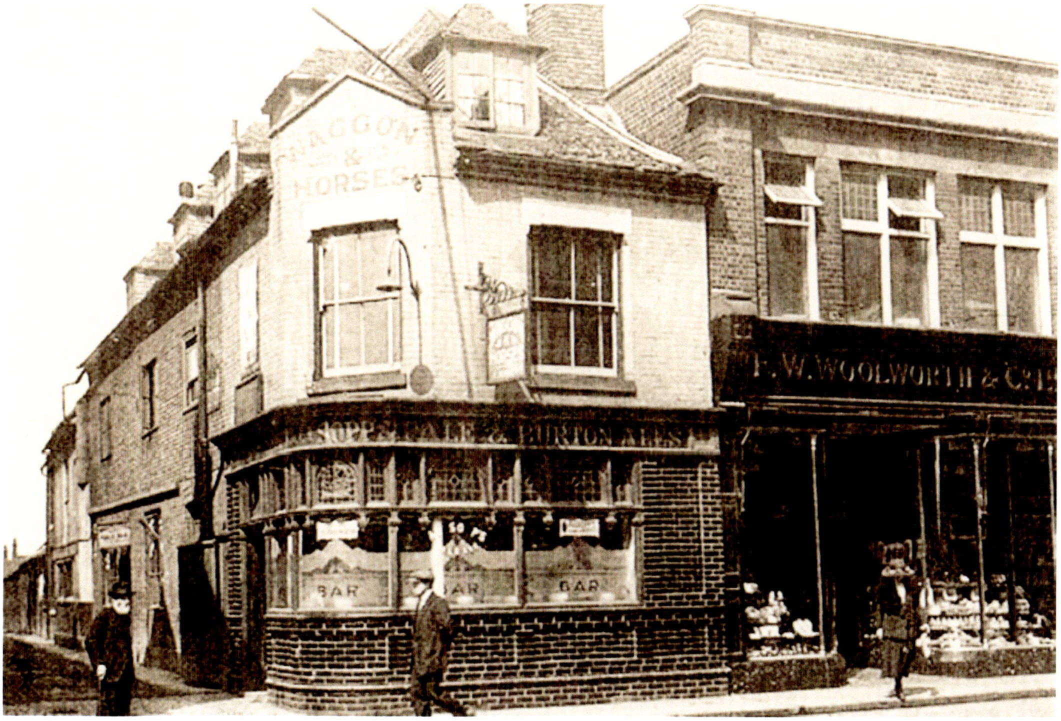

Waggon & Horses, *c.* 1927.

Londoners Flock to Live in Our City

In 1967, Peterborough was designated as a New Town. The Peterborough Development Corporation, under the fourteen-year leadership of Wyndham Thomas, collaborated with the city and county councils to transform Peterborough into one of the government's New Towns, aimed at alleviating the population pressure on London. The first township developed was Bretton, followed by the Ortons, which included Orton Goldhay, Orton Malborne, Orton Brimbles and Orton Wistow.

Peterborough became a home for people and businesses that were being encouraged to move out of London due to overcrowding in the capital. It became a location not only for individuals to settle but also an industrial and commercial office investment. Companies such as Pearl Assurance and Thomas Cook relocated to the city due to its good rail links and relatively low cost of land. Manufacturing, particularly engineering, and increasingly distribution businesses gravitated towards the city.

Among the other triumphs at this time was the creation of Nene Park (including Ferry Meadows), the parkway system and Queensgate Shopping Centre, which opened in 1982 with its flagship John Lewis store.

Before it was shut down by the government in the early 1990s, the Development Corporation created 26,000 new houses, 25,000 new jobs and 26 miles of new parkway. The population increased by 50,000 during this time and the city witnessed Lynch Wood business park being opened by Elizabeth II in 1988. Showcase Cinemas also came to the city.

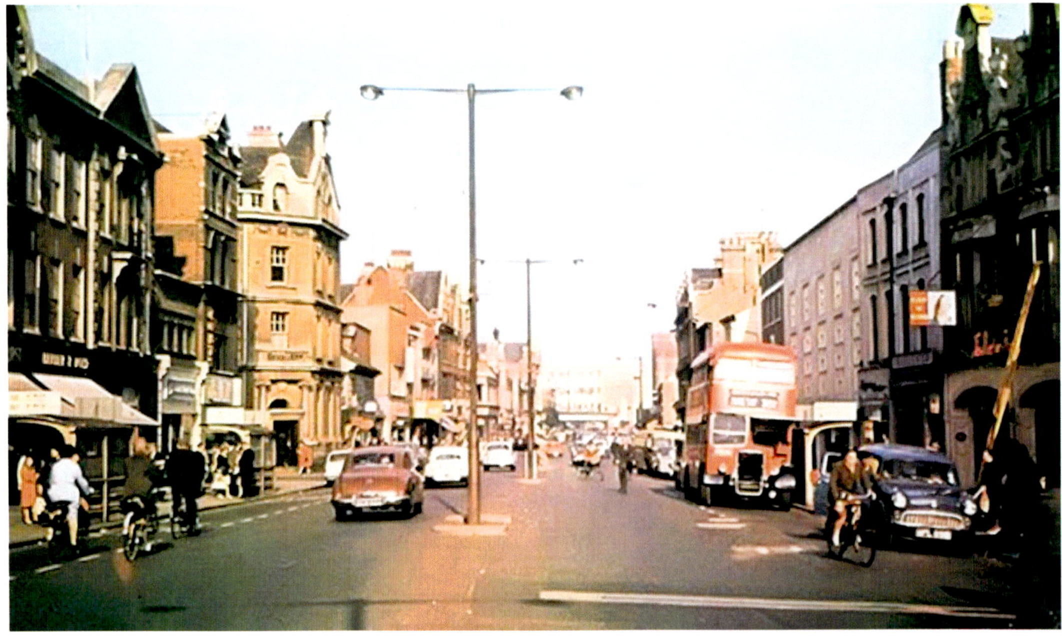

Long Causeway in the 1960s.

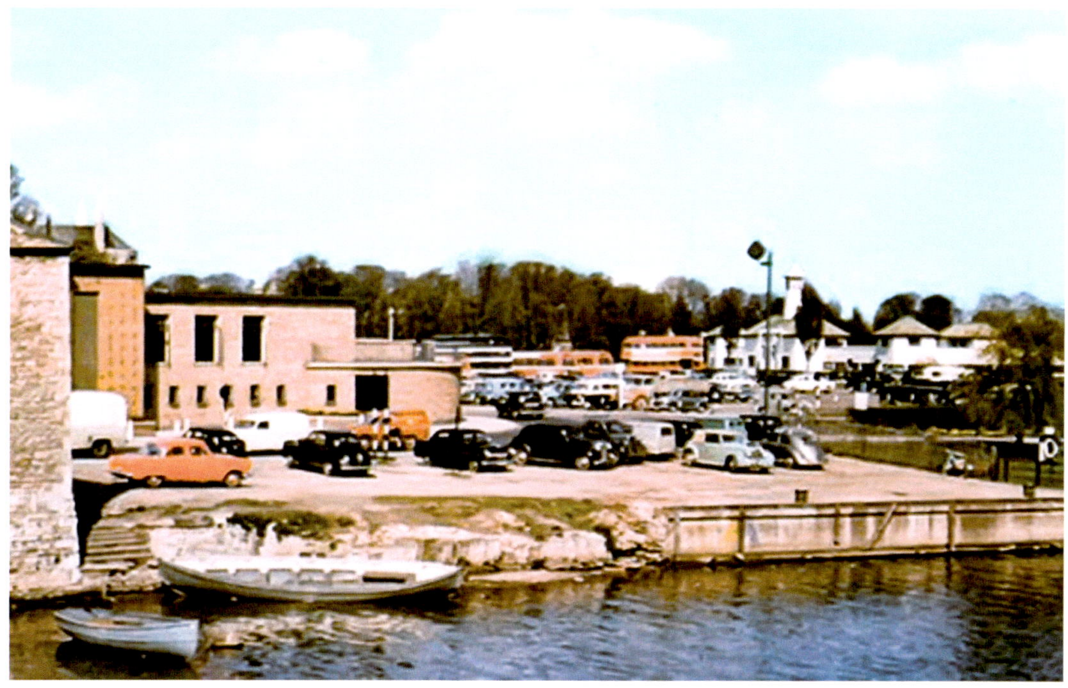

View from the city's bridge, 1960s.

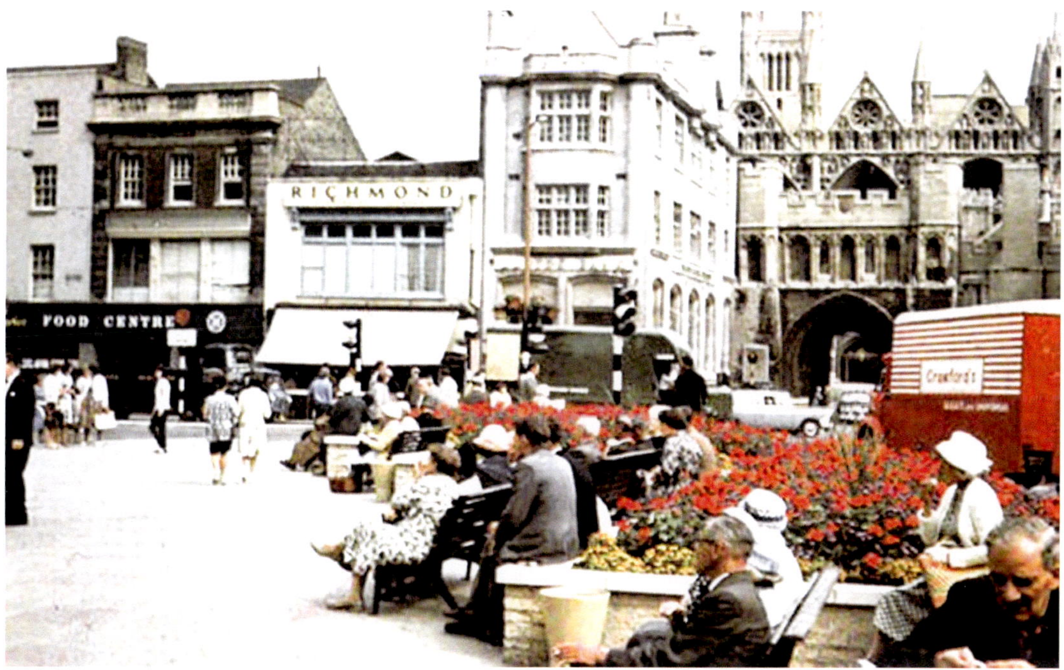

The city centre in the 1960s.

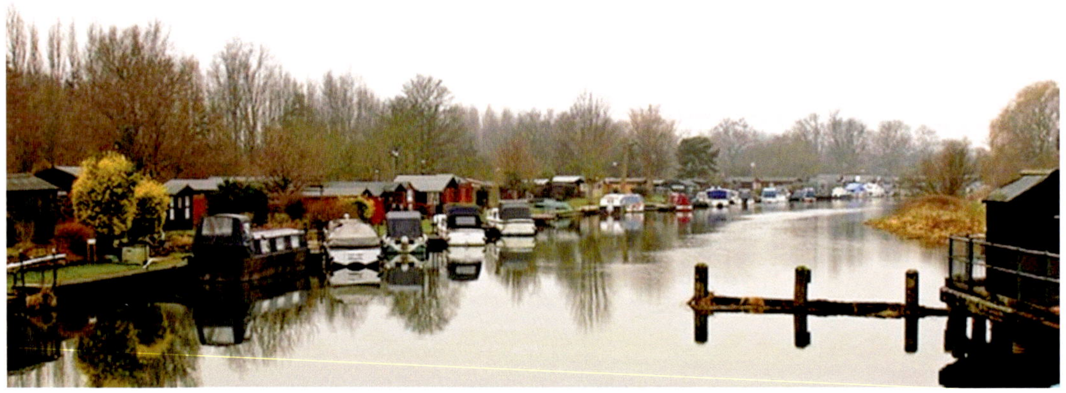

Boats moored along the River Nene at Nene Park, Ferry Meadows, in the 1970s.

In March 2015, Wyndham Thomas was made freeman of the city at the age of ninety in recognition of his fourteen years in charge of the development corporation. Sadly, in 2019 Wyndham passed away at the age of ninety-five, but he left an indelible mark on the growth and success of our city.

Peterborough's Hollywood Film Producer and Director

Born in Peterborough on 4 March 1941, Adrian Lyne was raised in London and studied at Highgate School, where his father taught. Adrian transitioned to filmmaking after briefly being a jazz trumpeter. He started by directing several short films before moving on to television commercials. This experience is said to have influenced his style as a feature film director, whose movies often explore themes such as romantic relationships, marital infidelity and the tension between reality and illusion.

Adrian debuted as a director with the 1980 film *Foxes*, which follows four teenage girls in the San Fernando Valley during the late 1970s. Jodie Foster played the sensible friend who tries to protect her peers from risky behaviours. While not a major commercial success, *Foxes* established Adrian's ability to portray sexuality appealingly to diverse audiences.

In 1983, the film *Flashdance* was produced, depicting a story about a young welder, played by Jennifer Beals, who pursues her aspirations of dancing on Broadway. The film highlights Adrian's use of visuals inspired by music videos. A song from the film's soundtrack, 'What a Feeling (Flashdance)', performed by Irene Cara, received several accolades. The music scores contributed to making *Flashdance* the third-highest-grossing film of 1983.

Adrian directed several notable films, including *9 ½ Weeks* (1986), *Fatal Attraction* (1987), which earned him an Oscar and a Golden Globe, *Indecent Proposal* (1993) and *Unfaithful* (2002). He was also involved in projects like

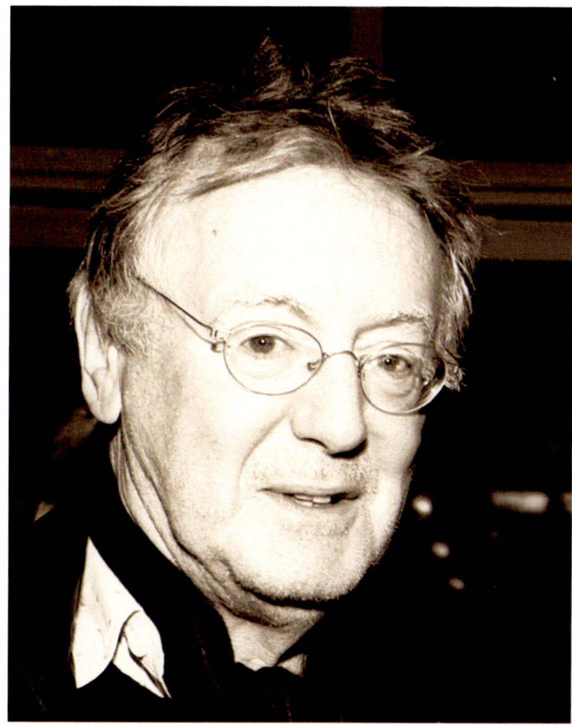

David Lyne.

'Stompanato', about Lana Turner and her relationship with mobster Johnny Stompanato, who was killed by Turner's daughter, Cheryl, in 1958.

Lyne worked on a film adaptation of Chuck Hogan's novel *Prince of Thieves* and co-wrote a remake of *Back Roads* in 2012. Based on Tawni O'Dell's 2000 bestseller, *Back Roads* follows a nineteen-year-old caring for his three sisters while his mother is jailed for killing their father. He becomes sexually obsessed with a neighbour, a mature mother of two. In 2022, Lyne directed the psychological thriller *Deep Water*.

Adrian has directed Oscar-nominated actresses Glenn Close, Anne Archer and Diane Lane. He focuses on portraying weak, vulnerable characters rather than heroes, aiming to disturb audiences and spark discussion with his films. His critics say he has an inbuilt inclination to make people laugh, cry and be horrified at the same time.

Certainly, Adrian is a Peterborian who has succeeded in achieving much notoriety in a career that was actually his second choice, having started out as a musician.

The Angel Hotel

The history of the Angel Hotel, on the corner of Bridge Street and Priestgate, goes back to the 1400s when the building held an important function in the town. It was originally a rest home in which visitors to the Benedictine monastery were entertained when there was no accommodation for them in the King's Lodging beside St Nicholas's Gateway.

The bailiff, who collected rents from townsfolk payable to the monks, recorded in his accounts for 1492 that the Angel hostelry had been added by the Abbot of Peterborough, William de Ramsey, to his private estates, which he had acquired for the maintenance of his household.

After the monastery had been dissolved, the front of the premises came into the ownership of the Fitzwilliams of Milton Hall. The rear part, the brewhouse, belonged to the Peterborough feoffees (governors of the city during the seventeenth and eighteenth centuries).

In 1673, its tenant was Thomas Deacon, founder of the charity school for boys. However, he does not appear to have been the landlord. A decade later, the property was described as 'a parcel of ground in Priestgate lane upon which a malt house, kiln, barns, stable and hogs sty are built which extends over the site of Wentworth Street'.

In 1730, the feoffees let the brewhouse to Earl Fitzwilliam, who acquired freehold of the entire premises by an exchange of property. Thus, the Angel Hotel formed part of the Milton estate.

As well as dinners, balls and other social events in connection with race meetings, cockfighting, etc., the Angel was an important place for functions. On 11 January 1738, the Peterborough Gentlemen's Society meeting was held there, and Vice President Edward Wortley Montagu MP was pleased to treat members

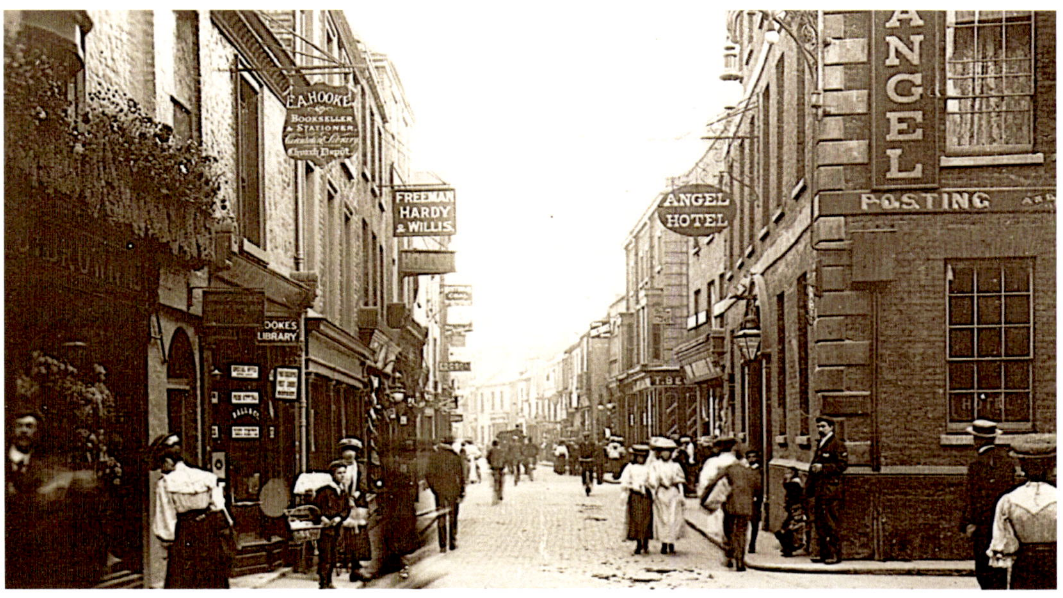

Angel Hotel, *c.* 1905.

to a strongman's performance by Mr Topham, who rolled up a large pewter dish and then bent a large poker around his neck. In April 1794, volunteers enrolled to become members of the Peterborough Corp of the Northamptonshire Yeomanry.

In the late 1920s and early 1930s, the Angel Hotel was remodelled, redecorated and fully refurbished to offer hot and cold water in all bedrooms, central heating was installed throughout and the public rooms were all brought up to standard, which included a dining room, restaurant, smoking room, lounge, reading and writing rooms, a large banqueting room and a magnificent ballroom. The lounge, with stained-glass windows, had great armchairs and the walls were decorated with desert scenes which enhanced this colourful room along with its blue ceiling dotted with stars and lighting effects, all of which gave the room its lush Eastern atmosphere. Reports at the time said it was simply délicieux!

The Angel Hotel had its own garage. Towards the end of the first quarter of the twentieth century it fell under the ownership of Paten & Co., who also owned two other hotels in Peterborough: the Grand and the Bull.

Today, WHSmith occupies the site of the Angel Hotel, which was demolished in 1972.

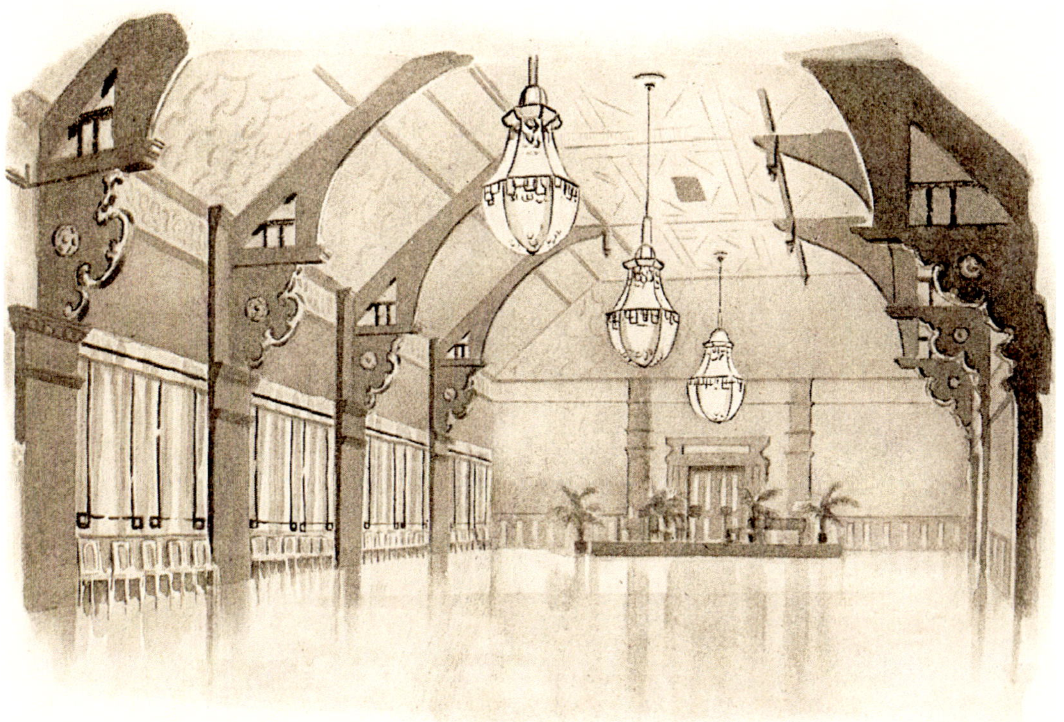

Sketch of the Angel Hotel's refurbished ballroom, *c.* 1935.

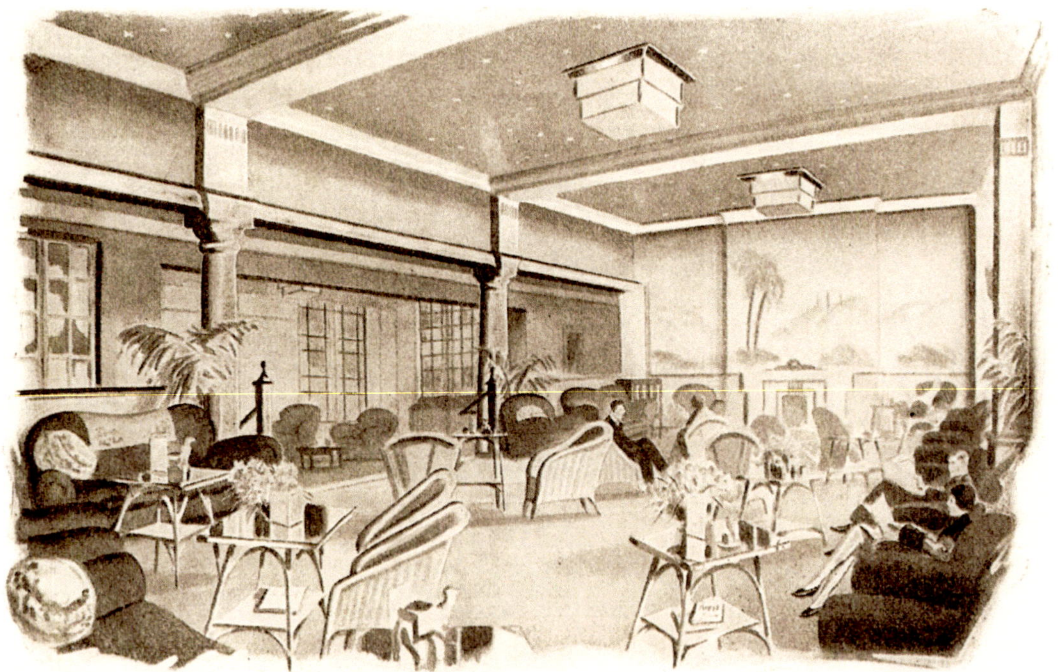

Sketch of the Angel Hotel's refurbished lounge, *c.* 1935.

Bob Geldof Lived Here

Born on 5 October 1951, Bob Geldof was brought up in Dún Laoghaire, Ireland. He was bullied at school and left Ireland to work as a slaughterman. He came to our city as a teenager when he worked in the pea-canning factory of Farrows & Co. in Fletton Avenue.

The Farrow & Co. canned vegetable business was sold to Batchelors of Sheffield, a Unilever subsidiary, in 1971. The Peterborough factory closed in 1973 with the loss of 250 jobs; production was relocated to Norwich. Premier Foods sold the Farrow's brand to Princes Foods of Liverpool in 2011, and Farrow's Marrowfat peas are still sold today.

After working and living in Peterborough for a brief spell, Geldof moved to work for the Princes Group in Wisbech, where canned and pouch products were produced. He is best known as a member of the Boomtown Rats. He helped organise the Live Aid and Live 8 events and formed the Band Aid charity group. Geldof also acted in the Pink Floyd film *The Wall*, a musical about the album of the same name.

He was married to Paula Yates from 1986 until their divorce in 1996. They had three daughters together. Paula later had a child with Michael Hutchence, the lead singer of INXS, who passed away in 1997. Following Paula's death in 2000, Geldof adopted their daughter, Tiger.

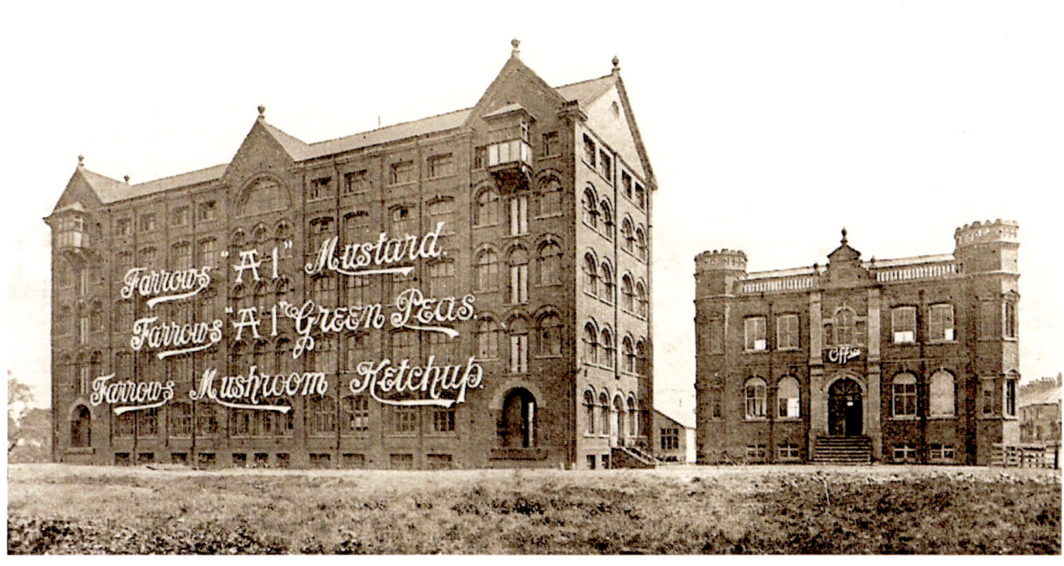

Farrows factory, Fletton Avenue, *c.* 1908.

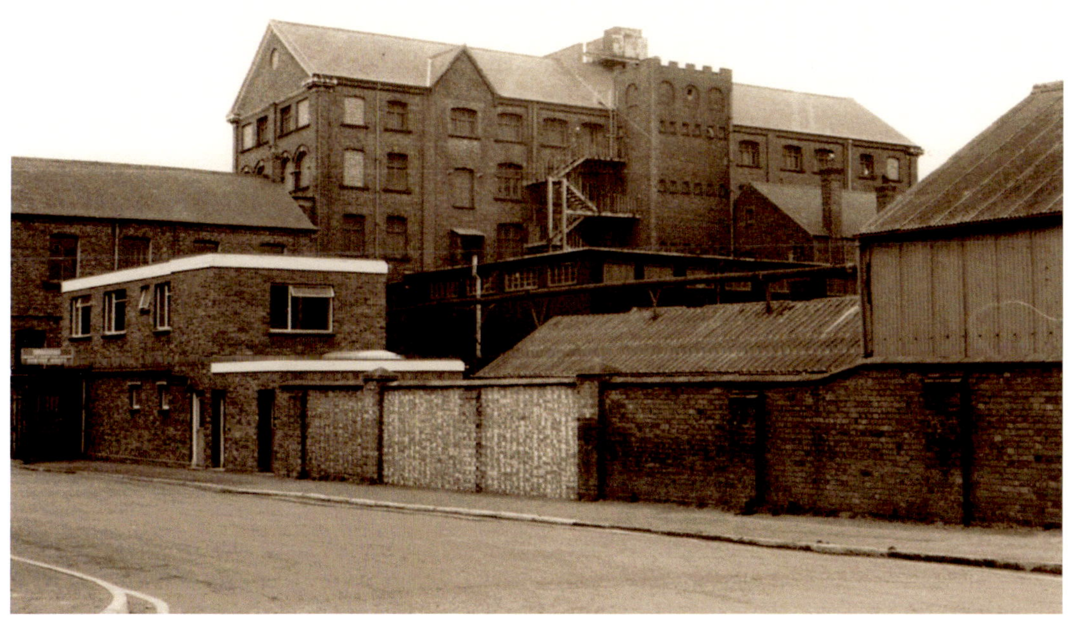

Rear of Farrows factory, *c.* 1972.

Geldof lives in London with his partner Jeanne Marine, a French actress. He was awarded an honorary knighthood in 1986 in recognition of his work in organising Band Aid and other concerts that raised millions for the starving people of Africa. Geldof is not a British citizen, however, so may never be called 'Sir'.

In 2006 and 2008, Geldof was nominated for the Nobel Peace Prize for his work on famine relief, but failed to get voted outright by the panel.

Fossils at Peterborough Museum

Our city was once over 50 meters under water and the seabed beneath was packed with clues from the past. Fossils dug from the limestone and clay give us vivid pictures of life in the Jurassic period.

Peterborough is one of the best places in the world to learn about this period, which saw an expansion in animal and plant populations. It was warm and watery 165 million years ago. A shallow sea covered the area and the climate was much warmer than today.

The Jurassic period ended 145 million years ago and lasted 54 million years. It is the middle period of the Mesozoic era, which covers all the time that dinosaurs were alive. The oldest fossils found are over 600 million years old.

Back then, Peterborough was much closer to the equator and together with warmer global temperatures the local climate would have felt balmy, much like the Caribbean today. Since the Jurassic period, the world's continents have moved hundreds of miles since the Earth formed billions of years ago, the rocky tectonic plates on its surface have moved around very slowly, powered by the heat of the Earth's core.

Fossils dug from local limestone and clay give a detailed picture of life in the region during the Jurassic period. A single partial skeleton (arms, legs, part of the backbone) was found in Peterborough and is one of the best examples of a sauropod from the entire UK.

Our brick pits have attracted fossil collectors and scientists from all over the world, but many of the best finds have been made by local people. They include Alfred Leeds (1847–1917) and his elder brother Charles, who collected near their family's farm at Eyebury, south of Peterborough. Alfred was entirely self-taught and amassed the largest collection of vertebrates in the world at his farm, where he would entertain visiting professional palaeontologists and scientists. An extinct fish, Leedsichthys, came to light in the Star Pit brick quarry in Dogsthorpe, Peterborough, and this and several other extinct species were named in honour of Alfred Leeds. The Leedsichthys was over 16 metres and is one of the largest fish ever known.

Another keen amateur palaeontologist was Alun Dawn (1923–2010), who specialised in the fossils of our area. A local man, he volunteered at the city's museum for thirty years and was the first recipient in 1990 of the Palaeontological Associations' Award for Amateur Palaeontologists. He discovered a nearly complete plesiosaur, plus a new one which was named after him.

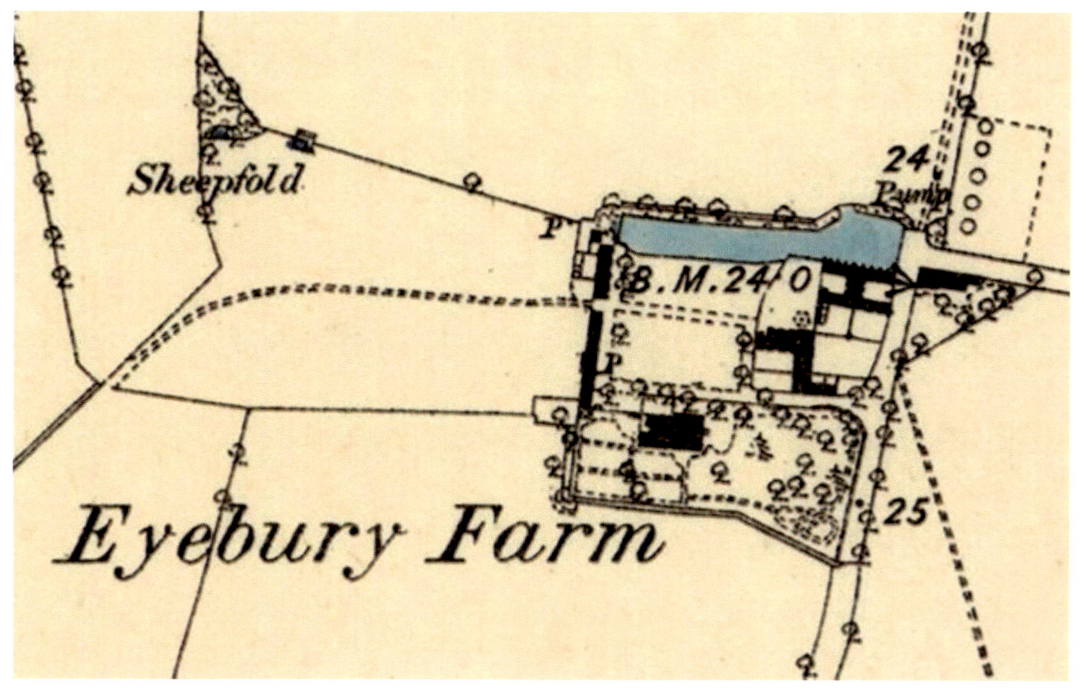

Above: Map *c.* 1900 of Eyebury Farm, where Alfred Leeds lived.

Right: Alfred Leeds, *c.* 1900. (Photo courtesy of the Leeds family)

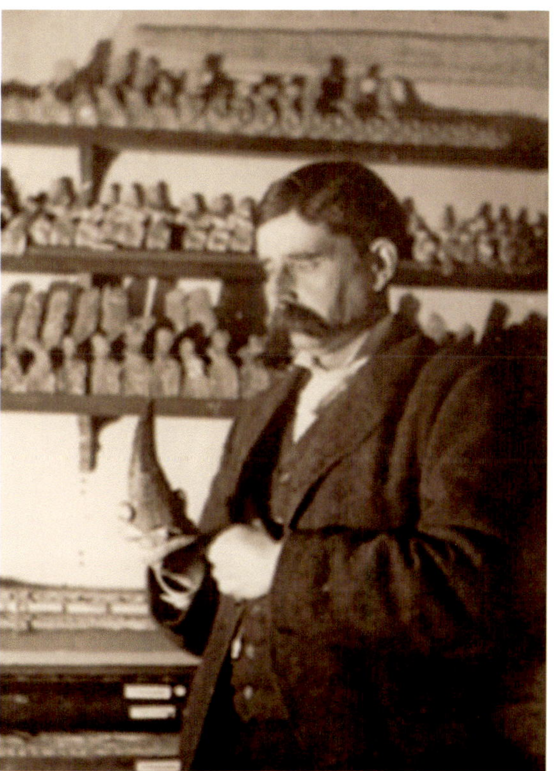

Alun made highly important discoveries and he and his team handled all the fossils and skeletons and assembled them for public display at our museum.

Our city has been blessed to have such specialists in their field as well as being a place renowned worldwide for unique fossils.

The Black Book of Peterborough

On 15 June 1215, King John of England signed a charter that would come to be known as the Magna Carta. It was drafted by the then Archbishop of Canterbury, Stephen Langton, and was an agreement to limit the rights of kings and make peace between the royal family and a group of rebel barons over taxation laws.

Since it was first signed by King John, the Magna Carta was reissued several times up until 1300 when King Edward I (King John's grandson) released the final version. Researchers say only seven editions have been found of the 1300 edition. The document is half a meter long and possesses the royal seal.

The Magna Carta provides the foundation for much of the justice system we have grown accustomed to today, including the stipulation that no one is above the law, not even the king, and that everyone has the right to a fair trial.

Magna Carta inspired the creation of several other documents, including the US Constitution and the Universal Declaration of Human Rights. Magna Carta was not really about the common person, but rather about the relationship between the barons and king; however, it became hugely important in later debates about civil liberties and the rights of ordinary people.

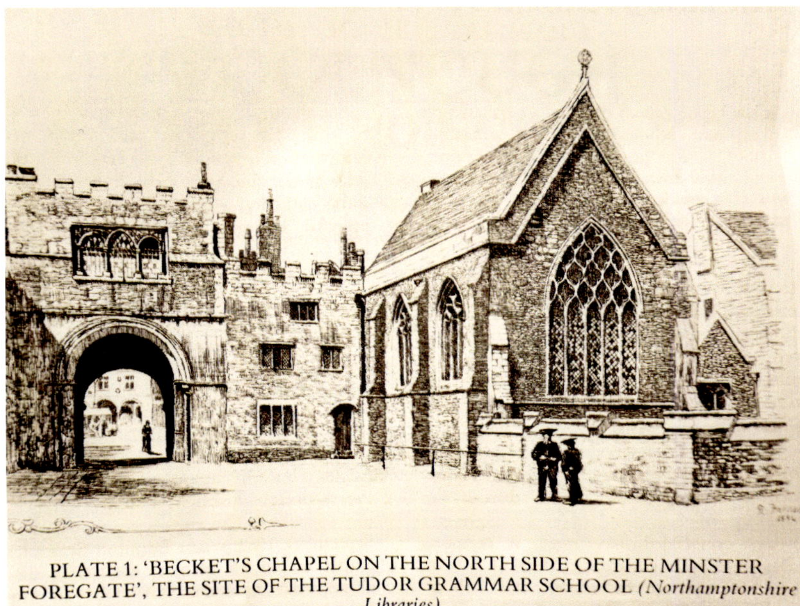

PLATE 1: 'BECKET'S CHAPEL ON THE NORTH SIDE OF THE MINSTER FOREGATE', THE SITE OF THE TUDOR GRAMMAR SCHOOL (*Northamptonshire Libraries*)

The King's Scholars of Peterborough Cathedral Grammar School.

The Black Book of Peterborough.

A copy of the Magna Carta in the Black Book of Peterborough (of twelfth- to fourteenth-century origin) gives us a glimpse of its early history. The copy found here was probably a discarded draft at the abbey, now the cathedral, and was in the possession of King's School, which was founded by King Henry VIII in 1541 as the Cathedral School to educate twenty poor boys. King's School was originally housed in Cathedral Precincts at the Becket Chapel. The curriculum consisted largely of Latin, Greek and Scripture.

The school governors had to look for other premises as the school grew, so they looked to purchase land for the new school in Thorpe Road but a fatal accident at the railway crossing caused them to think again and the current site was purchased on Park Road. The school was built by John Thompson, a renowned local and national builder as well as a former pupil. The new school opened on 30 October 1885 to boys only. It was not until 1976 that it became co-educational.

John Clare, Our Peasant Poet

John Clare is best known for being a romantic poet. He was born in July 1793 at Helpston village, 6 miles north of Peterborough, into a family of farm labourers.

His father's name was Parker Clare. John received little formal education and attended school until he was aged twelve.

Clare's family struggled to make ends meet, so the young John worked as a waiter, a gardener at Burghley House in Stamford, and a jobbing farmhand. Even undertaking these various odd jobs, he still had to accept parish relief for the poor.

Clare would often come to Peterborough to take a packet-boat on the River Nene to places like Wisbech. When Smith's Leam was cut it enabled river traffic to Guyhirn in 1728 and later navigation to Northampton in 1761. These trips enabled Clare to see more of the countryside at relatively low cost compared to a train journey from Peterborough, which was only possible from 1845.

In 1820, Clare married Martha (Patty) Turner, a milkmaid, but by 1823 the family were nearly penniless despite his poetry being published.

Facing financial and health issues, Clare published *The Rural Muse* in 1835. Despite positive reviews, it did not sell well enough to support him. Living with his wife and seven children, Clare's drinking and health problems worsened. He voluntarily entered a private asylum in Essex in 1837, escaped in 1841, but was later committed to St Andrew's asylum in Northampton that same year. There, he wrote his famous poem *I Am*, which was published in 1848.

Clare continued to write poems until 1864 when he died of a stroke at the age of seventy on 20 May at St Andrew's asylum, Northampton. He is buried at Helpston churchyard.

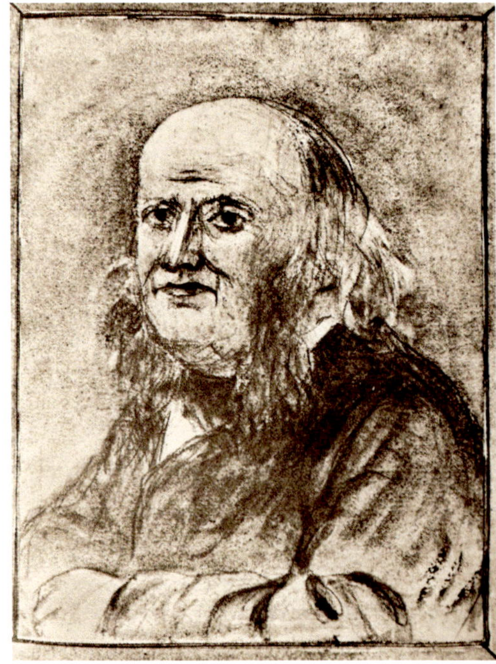

John Clare, the peasant poet.

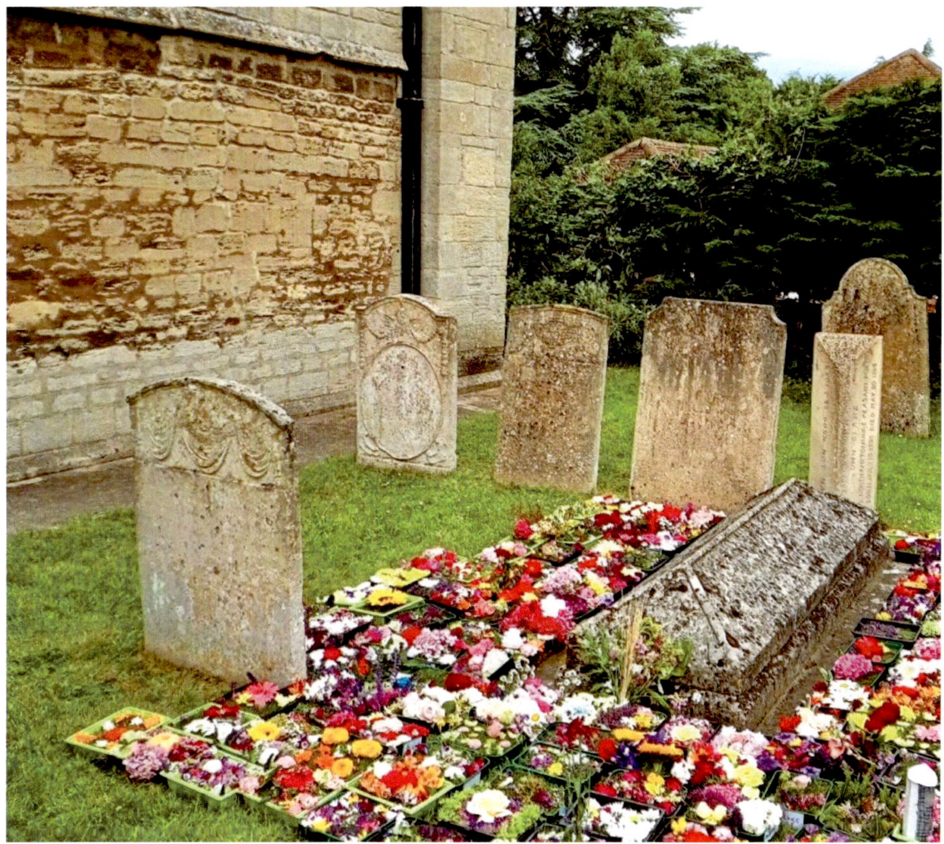

John Clare's grave at Helpston.

Driver of Peterborough's First and Last Tram

Our city's trams ran from 24 January 1903 until 15 November 1930. Public wheeled transportation has existed since the late 1850s, when the Great Northern Railway (GNR) established rail works in New England. Wagonettes operated between New England and the Market Place, now known as Cathedral Square, on market days and weekends. Although horse-drawn trams and tramline routes were considered at a council meeting in 1880, these plans were never implemented.

In 1896, horse-drawn omnibuses were introduced, and the Peterborough Omnibus Company operated routes between Long Causeway, Werrington, New England, Woodston, Fletton, Stanground, Farcet and Longthorpe. The stabling was located in Evan's Yard, off St John's Street. Each bus required eight horses for a day's work, with pairs being changed every two hours.

The British Electric Traction (BET) Company Ltd, the largest group in Britain, sought approval from the Light Railway Commissioners to operate light railways in the soke of Peterborough, city of Peterborough, and Woodston.

In 1899, powers were granted for tramlines to Walton, Dogsthorpe, Newark, Woodston and Stanground. However, plans for a line to Stanground and a circular route to Woodston were rejected due to the narrowness of Narrow Bridge Street and challenges in crossing the Great Eastern Railway line at the same level. Construction of the tramway began on 12 May 1902 by contractor JG White and Company Ltd. The track was 3 feet 6 inches wide and was laid as a single line with passing places to accommodate two tram cars.

Peterborough's electric tramway system was relatively small, with a maximum of fourteen cars and a track-watering car that could also be used as a snow plough.

In autumn 1902, local press representatives were invited to view the first tram car at the BET Company depot on Lincoln Road. The 3-foot 6-inch-gauge overhead wire system commenced operations on 24 January 1903 between Walton and Long Causeway, with the driver being Mr E. Jennings, followed a week later by a route to Dogsthorpe. Newark was reached on 28 March 1903, bringing the total route length to 5 miles.

The depot and offices were constructed on Lincoln Road at a cost of £3,000. The depot, featuring five roads converging to a single-line junction in Lincoln Road facing the city, utilised railway-type point levers for switching tracks. The cars, all open-topped, were supplied by BET at Loughborough and equipped with two motors, each with 17 hp, suitable for the city's level terrain. The first twelve tram cars accommodated twenty-two passengers inside and twenty-six outside on the top deck, on traversable wooden garden-type seats. Cars 14 and 15 (there was no number 13 due to superstition) were acquired in 1905 and

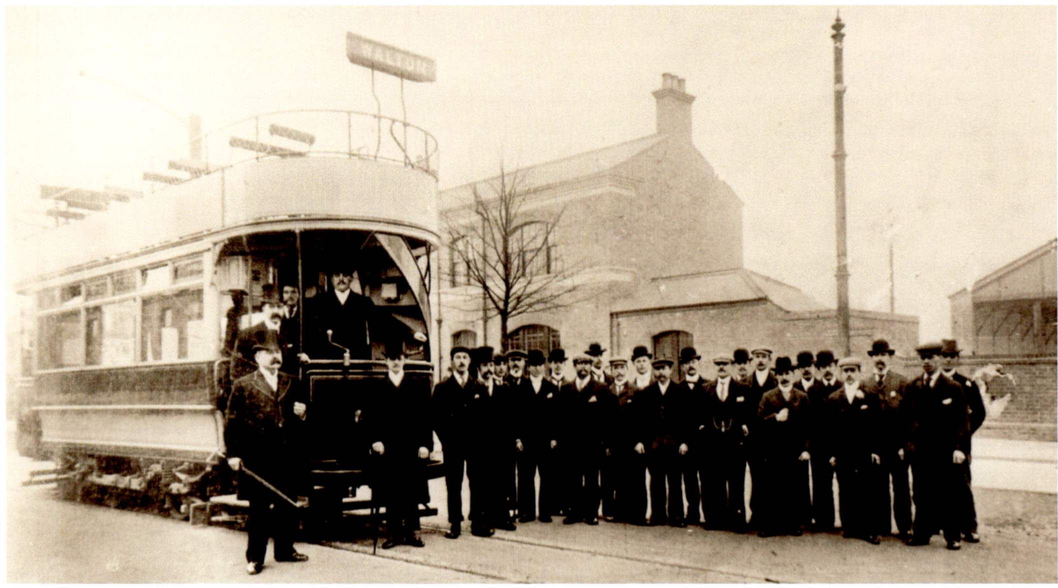

First tram outside Millfield depot in 1903.

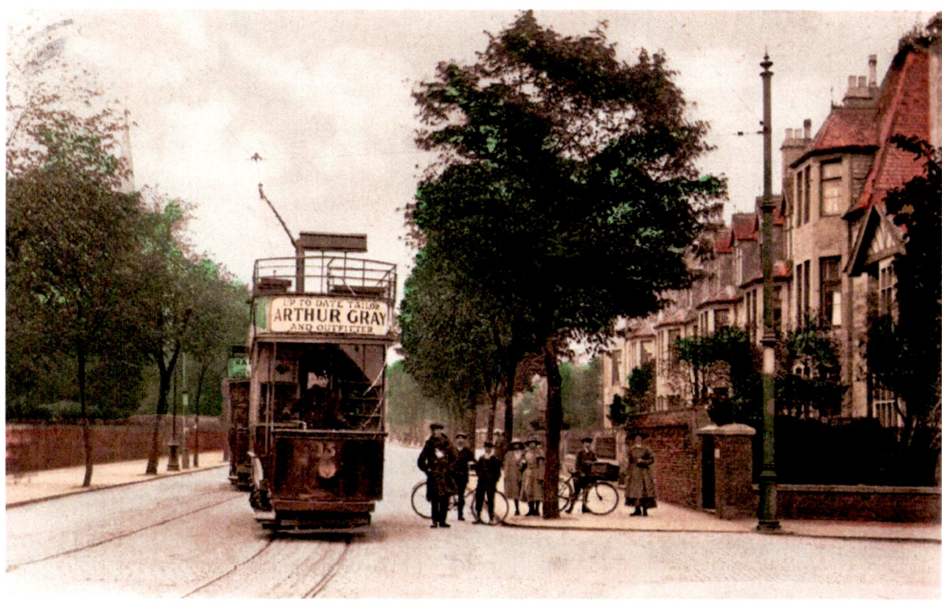

Tram on Lincoln Road, pictured at the corner of Fitzwilliam Street, *c.* 1923.

could accommodate twenty-eight passengers on top. The tram car livery was lake-brown and cream and then holly-green and cream.

During the First World War, women and temporary drivers were recruited, as in other towns and cities. During the General Strike of 1926, tram operations ceased completely. In 1930, BET Co. Ltd approached the city council to abandon the trams altogether. The last tram ran on 15 November 1930 with the driver, Mr E. Jennings, two conductors and ten passengers. Thus, Mr Jennings was the first and last driver of our city's trams.

Throughout twenty-seven years of service, the trams travelled 6–7 million miles and carried over 50 million passengers. By the early 1970s, all traces of tram standards had disappeared and the depot on Lincoln Road had become a bus depot. Double-decker buses replaced the various tram routes.

The local press reported the end of the city trams with statements such as: 'Our famous trams are no more. They came heralded by the whole populace. They went unhonoured and unsung, and all have gone to the Big Depot in the Sky.'

In recent years, trams have garnered renewed interest in many towns and cities due to their cost-effectiveness and environmental advantages.

Our Monastery Hospital

In around 1260, Abbot John built an infirmary for sick monks located in what is now the cathedral grounds. The arches of the aisles, as it was built like a church, still stand. It was in monasteries that the art of medicine was encouraged, as the monks had access to books. Learning about medical treatments then was very strange by today's standards. We can still read how they had some unusual recipes for medicines and patient care, but some of the herbs they used are the basis of various ointments and medicines used today.

The monks' herbarium was where the wall now runs between the Haven car park and the Bishop's Palace Garden. At this time the monks of Peterborough monastery lived according to the ideas of St Benedict, whose most famous monastery was founded in AD 500 at Monte Cassino, Italy, where much knowledge was gained from the Arab scientists of the Middle East and North Africa. Constantine of Africa had travelled there and retired to Monte Cassino around AD 800 to translate various works, including some on medicine. Not far away, in Salerno, a medical school and Europe's first university grew. Thus, the Benedictines had an ancient connection with medical matters long before they came to Peterborough with the Norman Conquest.

The monastic infirmary was also used to help sick travellers and the poor. Some forms of treatment were for special cases. In the Middle Ages, attention was given to leprosy. The Spital Bridge, over the railway north of Peterborough Station, is a reminder of St Leonard's hospital for lepers.

During the reign of Henry VIII, when he broke away from Rome and made monastery properties his own, the monks left Peterborough infirmary and the buildings were left to crumble.

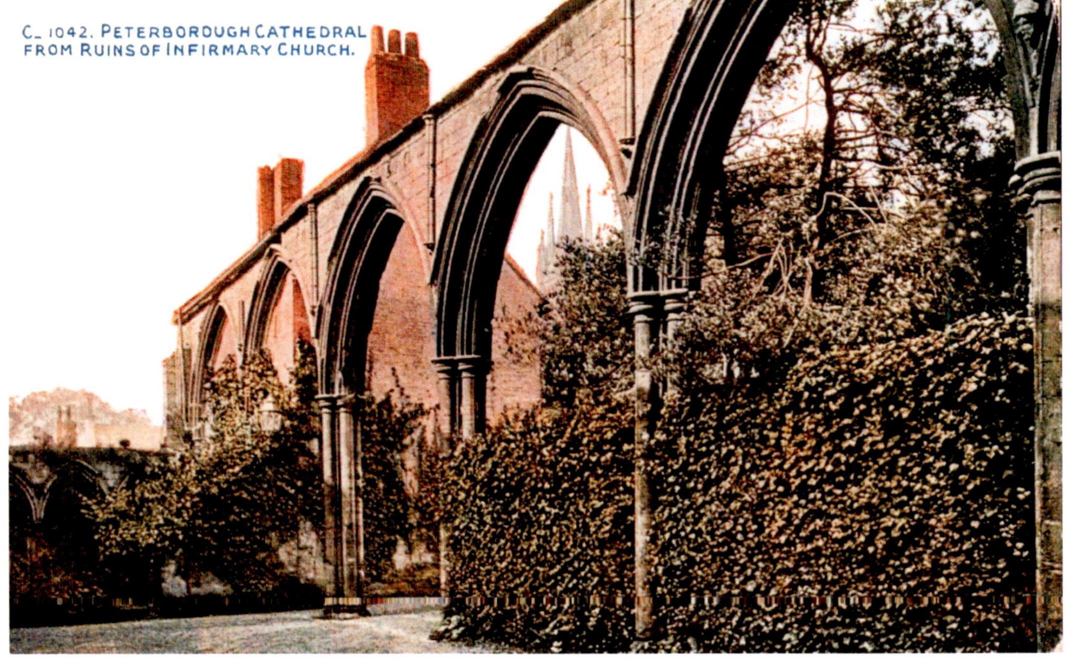

Postcard of the ruins of the monastic infirmary, dated 1907.

In 1665, plague raged in London, and in 1666 it appeared in Peterborough. In the early 1700s the feoffees, leading Peterborough citizens who were trustees that held a fief or fee, i.e., land for beneficial or charitable use on behalf of its owners, wrote to the MP for Peterborough, Mr Edward Wortley Montague of Hinchingbrooke, about the plight of the elderly poor. The latter secured a site in 1744 for the Wortley Almshouses in Westgate.

Later there were other almshouses in and around the city such as the one in Cumbergate, along with one at Paston Ridings. If the inmates of places like this were ill there were sometimes sick rooms for them and perhaps a local physician, surgeon or apothecary would call. Others were cared for in their own homes, as Peterborough was a small place and like many other towns it did not get a hospital until the nineteenth century.

Interestingly, great wars seem to have motivated interest in medical matters. This is not surprising given the appalling plight of the war wounded and many other victims, like the 1,500 French prisoners of war who died at Norman Cross, near Peterborough, during the long wars with Napolean. When the wars ended at Waterloo, the Peterborough Yeomanry disbanded and the funds that remained were used to set up a dispensary in Cowgate (the site now under Crescent Roundabout).

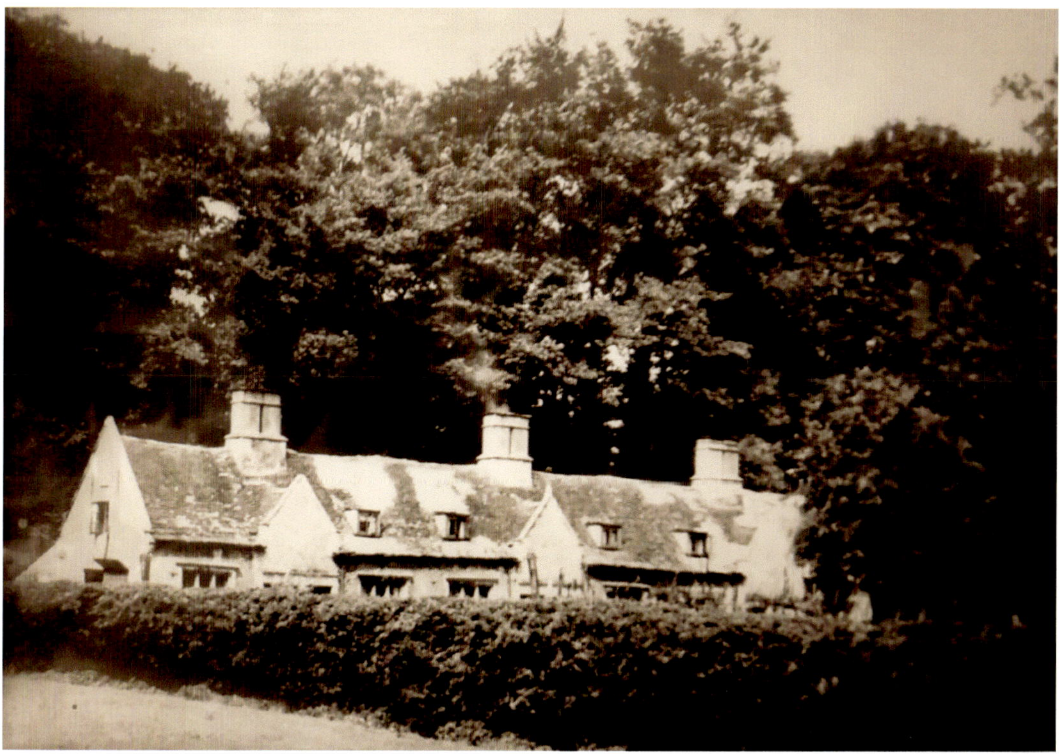

Paston Almshouse, Montagu Road, *c.* 1915.

Before long the Cowgate dispensary proved inadequate for the volume of people requiring medical assistance. In 1822, Lord Fitzwilliam presented a building in Milton Street which served the city and surrounding countryside until 1856 when Lord Fitzwilliam exchanged the Milton Street premises for a mansion in Priestgate. The building now houses the city's museum and art gallery. The latter infirmary served Peterborough for seventy years, supported by voluntary subscriptions and collections like Hospital Saturday carnival parades.

An interesting aside is that a young man who had been a pupil at Peterborough Infirmary in Priestgate, St Clair Thompson, later worked in London as a house surgeon to Sir Joseph Lister, who amongst other things pioneered antiseptic surgery. The latter practice of antiseptic surgery prevented many deaths due to infection. By coincidence, it was St Clair Thompson's elder brother, Dr William, who was Peterborough's first Medical Officer of Health, 1837–81.

Our Guildhall Is an Exact Replica of Amsterdam's

The current building replaced a medieval guildhall situated on the northern side of the Market Place, renamed Cathedral Square in 1963. Local people were determined to erect a new structure to commemorate the restoration of the monarchy, King Charles II, in 1660. Previously there had been a single-storey market cross on the present Guildhall site from at least 1613.

The existing Guildhall was partly or completely rebuilt in 1671 by builder John Lovin, a mason contractor from Peterborough, and a room was erected over the old piazza. It is built in the classical style and is very similar in design to the old Town Hall in Amsterdam before it was burnt down and demolished to make way for the Palace on Dom Square.

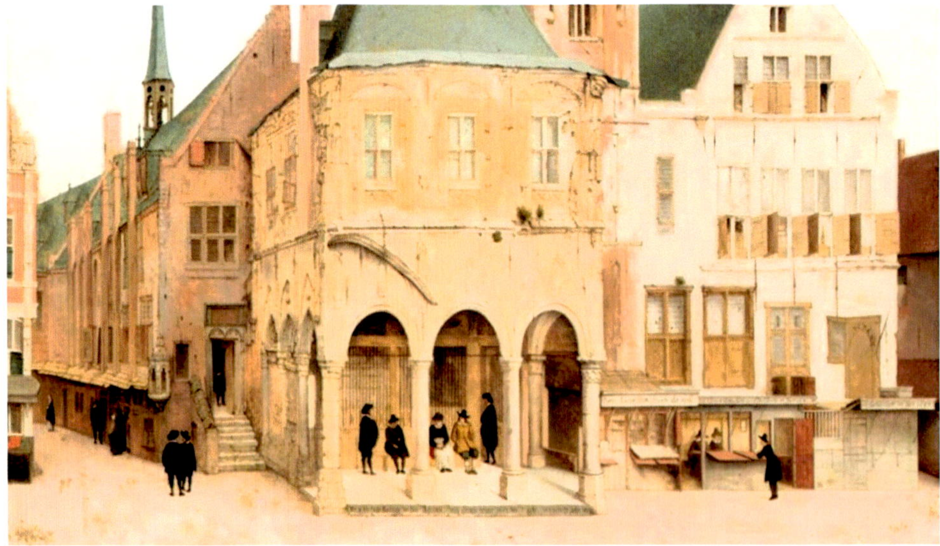

Amsterdam Guildhall.

The Peterborough feoffees, or parish trustees, who held investments and were responsible for collecting and distributing income each year, along with the city governors, were the local authority or body undertaking the erection of the Guildhall and its subsequent maintenance.

The cost of erecting the 1671 building was defrayed partly by public subscription, partly by a donation from Lord Fitzwilliam, who controlled the local Parliamentary elections, and finally by an issue of specially struck Peterborough halfpence coins.

The Guildhall was first erected as a court room for Quarter Sessions held by the Magistrates of the Liberty of Peterborough. At the end of the eighteenth century the upper room was used as a school room by the headmaster of Anne Ireland's charity school, which was controlled by the Peterborough feoffees. Public meetings, concerts, and puppet shows were sometimes held in the room. Also, the high bailiff of the dean and chapter, who had the right of returning members to serve in Parliament, held meetings in the Guildhall room for the nomination of candidates.

When Peterborough was incorporated (i.e., given city status) in 1874 the Guildhall was used as a Council Chamber and offices of the local authority were in the adjacent buildings. The latter building subsequently became the police station.

The open space under the Guildhall was used for the sale of butter and eggs. The Peterborough feoffees received the rents for stalls under the cross – though the cathedral dean and chapter collected all other tolls from the stallholders in the adjoining Market Place, now Cathedral Square.

In 1930 new municipal buildings were erected in Bridge Street and meetings in the Guildhall were discontinued. The new Town Hall in Bridge Street was officially opened by Alderman Whitsted on 16 October 1933.

Other interesting events that have occurred in or in connection with the Guildhall include the building being scheduled as an ancient monument in 1928 when it was completely restored by the city corporation under the advice of the Society for the Preservation of Ancient Buildings.

A fine carving of the arms of King Charles II appears beneath the gable of the east front, beneath which are the arms of the bishop and dean in 1671, the arms of Sir Humphrey Orme (chairman of the governors) and Peterborough's MP from 1654 to 1671, along with the Montagu family who had considerable political influence in the city during the seventeenth and eighteenth centuries.

In 1957 Peterborough became twinned with Bourges in France. A plaque depicting the Bourges coat of arms can be seen on the east side of the Guildhall. Today, the upper room is unused, but the open space below provides a venue for civic, art and cultural events.

Earlier this century the city council proposed a scheme whereby the ground floor would be enclosed by glass, but this was abandoned due to the cost.

On 4 July 2012, the Guildhall was the starting point for the Olympic flame's Day 47 journey before leaving for Lincolnshire as part of the UK relay tour in preparation for the 2012 Summer Olympics.

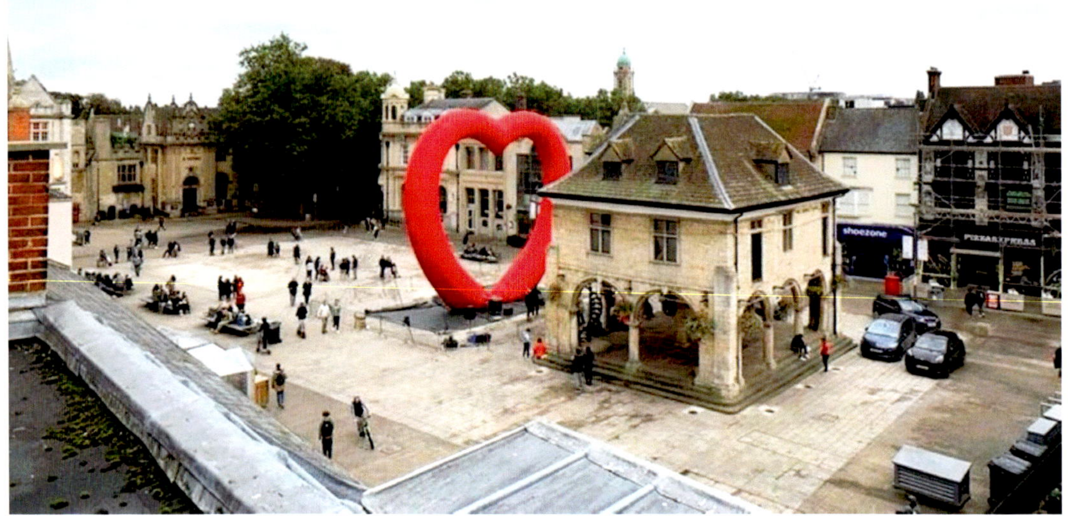

Our Guildhall, *c.* 2023.

Britain's Most Ethically Minded Community

In 1992, the Co-operative Bank took the pioneering step to become the first UK bank to launch a customer-led ethical policy, giving customers a say on the issues that are important to them.

In 2002, the bank declared Peterborough as Britain's most ethically minded community. A survey of the bank's customers showed that Peterborough people exhibited the greatest enthusiasm for ethical issues, including climate change, ethical investment, nuclear weapons, lending policy and director's remuneration. Our city beat Oxford and Manchester. London came seventh; Leicester was tenth.

At the time bank spokesperson Simon Williams said, 'We are famous for asking our customers what we should do with their money. This is the fourth time in ten years that we've asked our customers to vote on ethical issues and in 2002 we've had a record number of responses. The research shows people are generally more supportive of our ethical stance than ever before, giving us an overwhelming mandate to maintain our policies.'

The most recent poll in 2024 identified that support for local communities, support for co-operatives and environmental protection remained high. Other issues that were deemed important to people included the conduct of the bank in terms of not banking, investing in or lending to companies that are involved in the unsustainable exploitation of natural resources; not banking, investing in or lending to companies that manufacture chemicals that endure in the environment

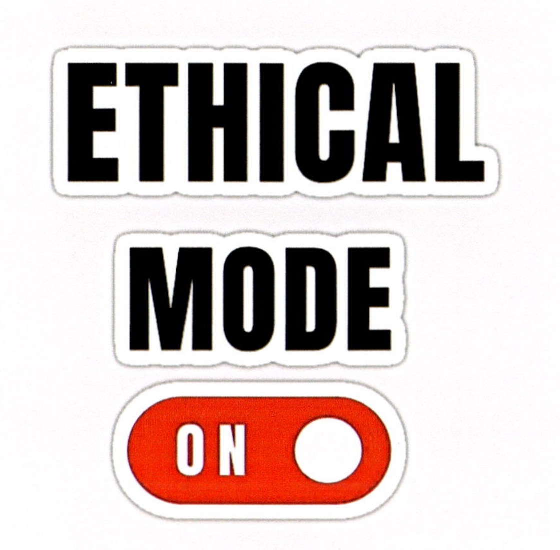

Ethical sticker.

or are harmful to health; and supporting companies that invest in renewable energy.

In January 2025, Coventry Building Society completed the acquisition of the Co-operative Bank that was established in 1872. Both banks still trade under their individual names.

The Peterborough UFO Scare

The wave of sightings of the so-called phantom unidentified flying objects over the British Isles during the spring of 1909 might have remained unknown had it not been for Chales Fort, who in 1931 came across this information as he was undertaking research at the British Library: he stumbled across a brief description of a UFO sighting by a Peterborough police constable. Fort continued to document additional sightings reported in the newspapers of that era, as well as the efforts made to dismiss these airship observations as mere products of delusion and hysteria.

On the night of Tuesday 23 March 1909, PC Kettle saw a strange, cigar-shaped craft passing over the city centre. One Miss Gill also reported seeing bright lights above Peterborough's St John the Baptist Church. The account given by PC Kettle was substantiated by the testimonies of Mr Banyard and Mrs Day from March, Isle of Ely, who independently observed a similar event two nights later. In fact, these incidents were the prelude to several dozen sightings throughout April and May 1909, mostly in East Anglia and South Wales. As the *London Standard* newspaper reported in May: 'There seemed to be common features to the various eyewitness accounts with few exceptions they all speak of a torpedo-shaped object, possessing two powerful searchlights.'

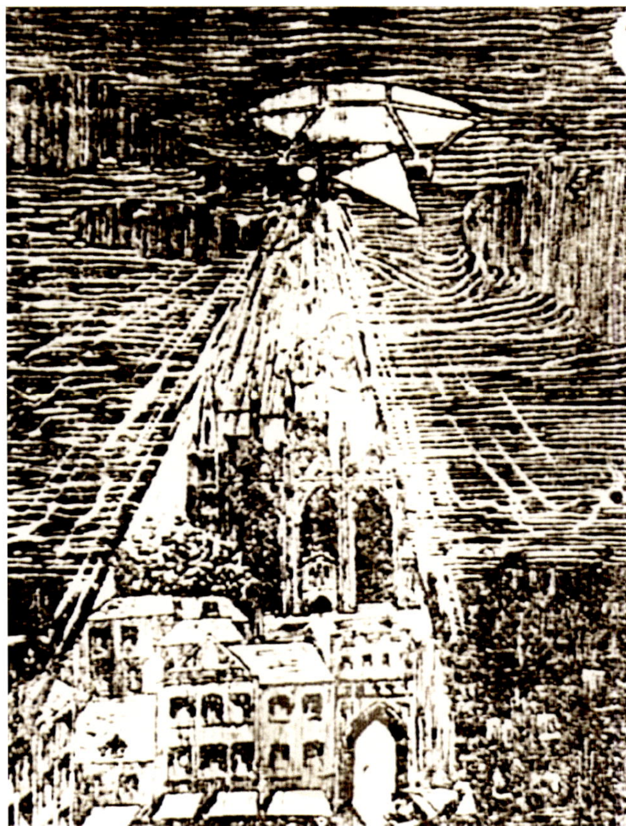

Artist's recreation of the airship that appeared in the *Peterborough Advertiser* on 27 March 1909.

The rigid airship called the Zeppelin was invented by Ferdinand von Zeppelin and was patented in Germany in 1895 and in the United States in 1899. During the First World War, the German military undertook numerous bombing raids on Britain which resulted in over 500 deaths. After the war, the lifting of restrictions on airship construction permitted the initiation of work on the Graf Zeppelin. During the 1930s, airships such as the *Hindenburg* and new models of the Graf Zeppelin conducted regular transatlantic flights from Germany to North America and Brazil. Eventually, safety issues associated with hydrogen, plus the operational difficulties of such huge airships, along with the rapid advancements of airplane technology led to the gradual decline of airships in civilian aviation and military use. Could the UFO sightings back in 1909 actually have been Zeppelins?

The Clock with No Face and the Monk's Stone

The Peterborough Cathedral clock was the oldest working clock mechanism in the world when it was replaced in 1950. The striking train housed within the main wooden frame is thought to date back to 1350. However, in the considered opinion of Michael Lee, who undertook its restoration after its removal from the tower in 1986, it is more likely to date back to 1450. This would coincide with the cathedral records where first mention of a clock is a reference to Richard the Clocksmith in 1452.

Further mention of the clock comes in 1687: '31 January received from Mr Standish ye sum of Seven Pounds for repairing and turning ye Clock into a pendulum and to have two pounds more if it be approved by Mr Patrick and Mr Turner … rec'd by me John Watts.'

This was a couple of years after Galileo found that a pendulum gave a regular beat and such a clock kept accuracy to within a few seconds per day. The 1686 John Watts timekeeping movement was replaced with a fine timekeeper, painted blue, signed 'Jno Wilson Fecit 1836'. The clock is now on display in the north choir aisle.

The Monk's Stone, or the Hedda Stone, can be found behind the main altar of Peterborough Cathedral, in an alcove of the Lady Chapel. This Saxon carving has survived from the original Saxon monastery and was thought to date from the late 800s but is now suspected to be even older. The carvings are said to depict Jesus Christ and some of the early Christian saints. Jesus is the central figure, with a cross in the halo around his head. On the left stands his mother, the Virgin

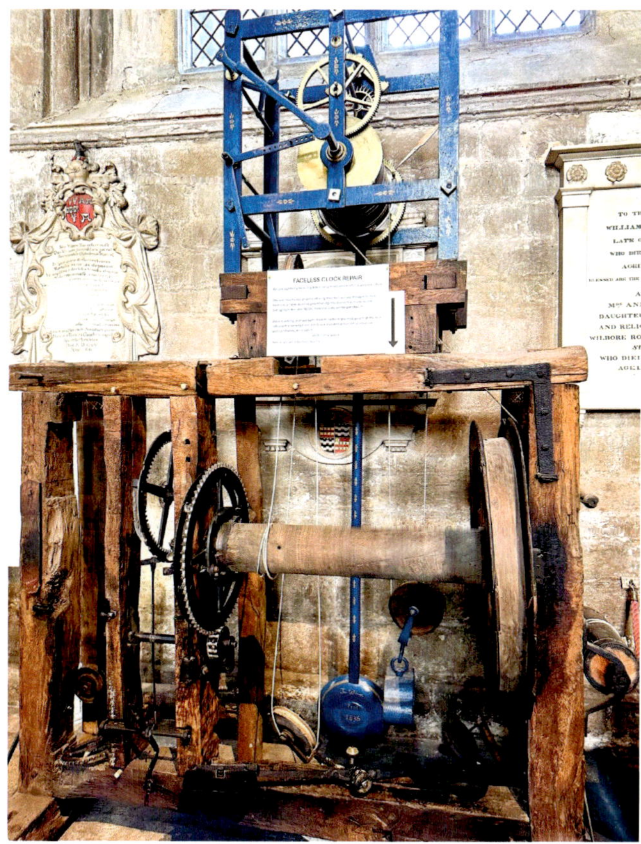

Peterborough Cathedral's clock with no face, *c.* 2024.

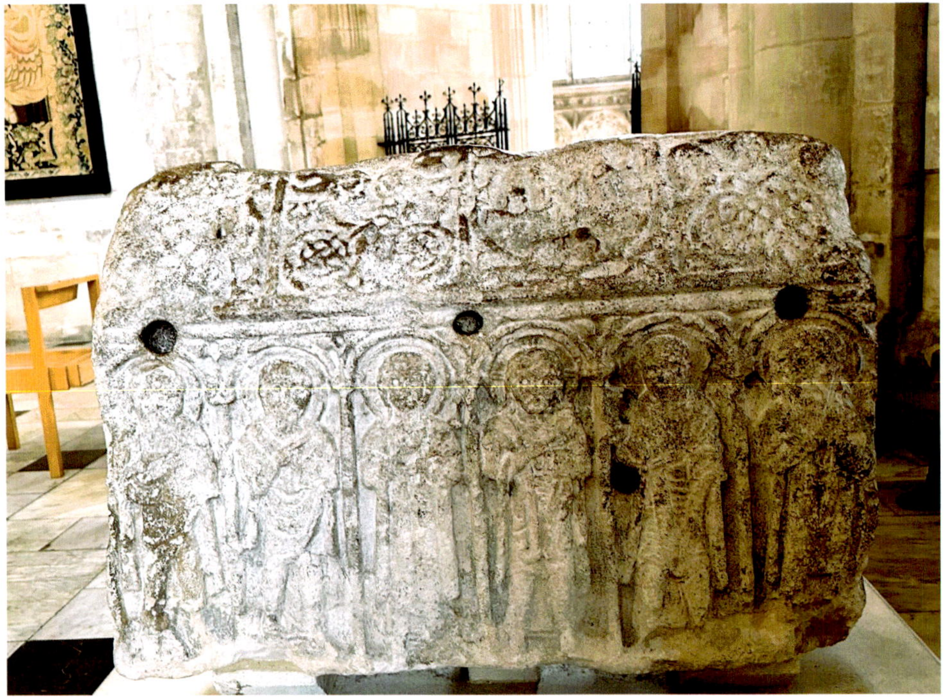

Peterborough Cathedral's Hedda Stone.

Mary, holding a lily, which symbolises purity. On the right is St Peter, holding the keys of Heaven. They stand under classical arcading and wear Roman-stye clothing, but the panels of interlaced patterns and birds above the figures suggest a northern European influence.

There are differing interpretations regarding the significance of the stone. Some scholars believe that the figures represent twelve monks who were killed during the Danish raids, which claimed the lives of approximately eighty-four monks, including Abbot Hedda.

Accidents, Suicides and Murders Come to Our Railways

Peterborough has had several railway stations over the years. Peterborough East operated from 1845 to 1966, while the current station opened in 1850 and was previously known by various names, including Peterborough North and briefly Peterborough Crescent from 1858 to 1866. The latter name was derived from the crescent of Georgian houses that once stood where Crescent Bridge is now located.

For men, women, children, workers, pedestrians and passengers the railway brought both life and death, with tragic accidents, suicides and murders. The oldest to die was eighty-six-year-old Juliana Ireland, who was hit by a train at Peterborough East in 1887. The youngest was sixteen-month-old Frederick

Harris, who wandered onto the tracks at Woodcroft Castle, near Peterborough, in 1857.

Railway staff were most often the victims. In 1865, a boiler explosion at New England's railway works killed three men. A plaque in St Paul's Church on Lincoln Road in New England, Peterborough, commemorates twenty-one Great Northern line workers who died between 1871 and 1891, though only seven deaths occurred within the city. The 200 recorded inquests likely understate the true number of Peterborough railway workers killed.

The railway often transported unsettling cargo. In 1896, a cleaner found a newborn's body in a carriage. This was the third such incident that year; another baby was mailed to a Peterborough hotel, and in 1869 a deceased baby was found in a labelled hamper in a first-class ladies' waiting room.

Fatalities on the railway prompted considerations for change. In 1880, Marion Ann Dunn was killed at the Crescent level crossing outside Peterborough North Station. Although the crossing gates were centrally locked, she managed to bypass the lock and entered the path of an oncoming goods train, which she could not see due to another train passing by. Her two children witnessed her death. Following this accident, her family campaigned for a bridge. While there was initial opposition, a subway was constructed as an interim measure, and eventually the Crescent Bridge was completed and officially opened in 1913.

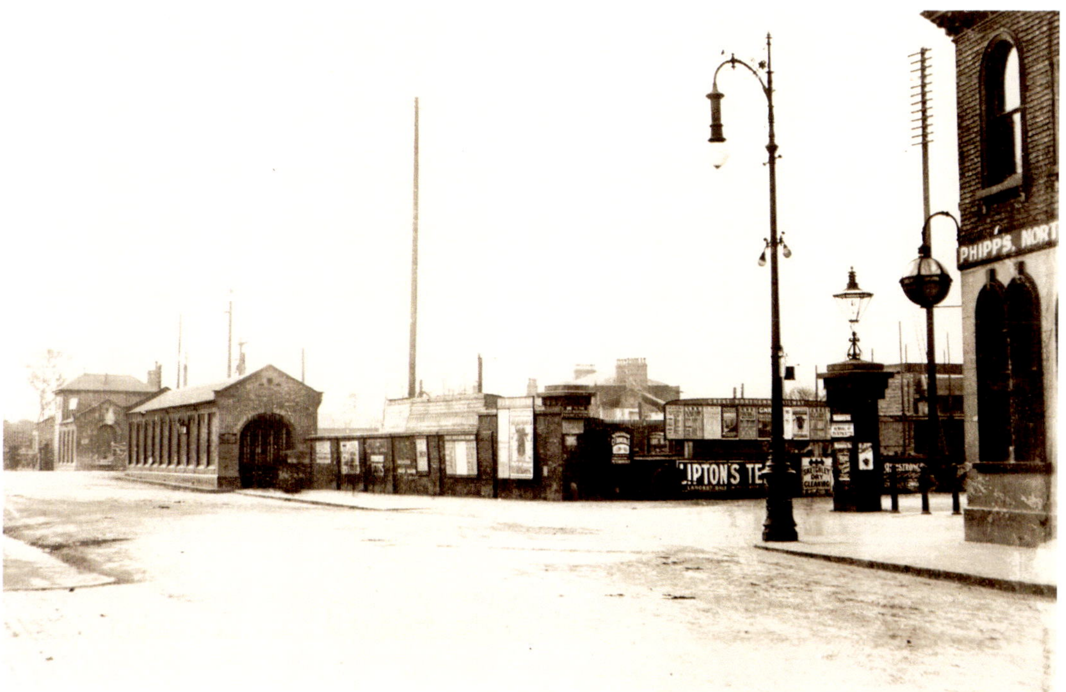

Railway subway, *c.* 1912.

The Wild Hunt and Black Shuck

The earliest documented reference to Black Shuck dates to the year 1127, found in the *Peterborough Chronicle*. It recounts that on the Sunday following Abbot Henry's arrival to Peterborough from Poitou, France, many people witnessed a group of ghostly huntsmen in the deer park of Peterborough and in the woods that stretched to Stamford. These huntsmen were described as black, huge, hideous and menacing, riding on black horses with hounds that had jet-black fur and red eyes. Witnesses reported that approximately twenty to thirty of these entities remained in the area from Lent until Easter, spanning a duration of around fifty days.

The accounts in the *Peterborough Chronicle* are considered the first written descriptions of ghost dogs resembling Black Shuck, or a large dog the size of a calf or small horse. Additionally, the *Chronicle*'s mention of spectral huntsmen and hounds aligns with the folklore concept of a 'Wild Hunt', which is a European legend viewed as a bad omen.

Although the *Peterborough Chronicle* dates from 1127, it is likely that the legend of Black Shuck existed in oral tradition even earlier. In the late ninth and early tenth centuries, Vikings from Scandinavia settled in East Anglia, bringing with them Norse mythology. This influence is evident in early Anglo-Saxon literature, such as the epic *Beowulf*. It is possible that the folklore of Black Shuck has origins in the tales of Geri and Freki, the wolves associated with the Norse god Odin.

Despite these ancient origins, sightings of Black Shuck have been reported in East Anglia up to the present day. The region is known for its overcast climate

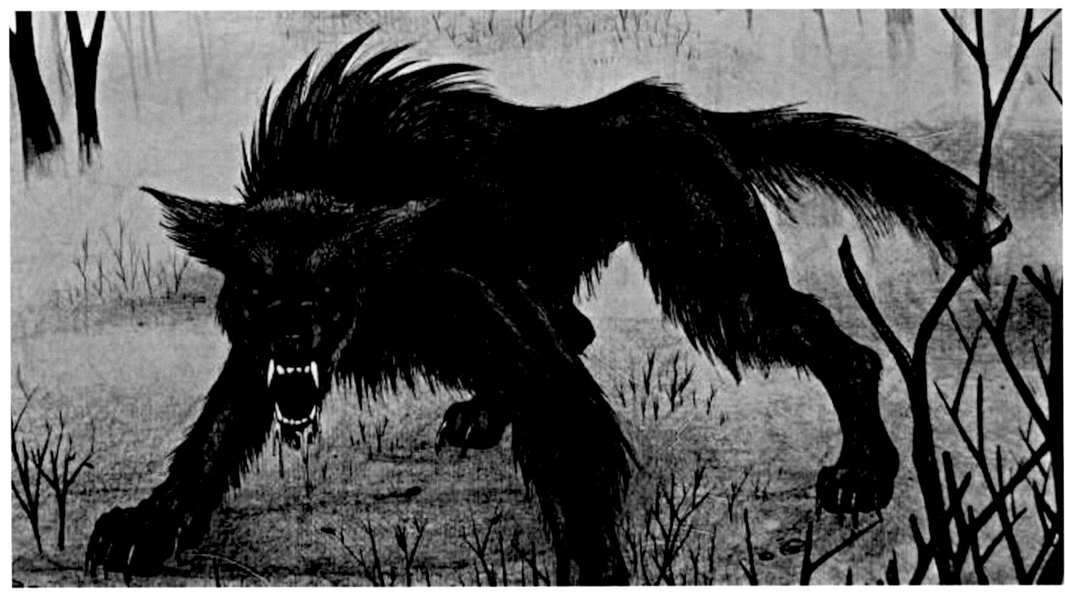

Black shuck.

and peat farming in marshy areas of the Fens. Some suggest that the legend of Black Shuck inspired Conan Doyle's *Hound of the Baskervilles*, noted for its gloomy setting.

1816: The Year Without a Summer

On 10 April 1815, Indonesia's Mount Tambora erupted, drastically reducing its height by 4,200 feet, or 1,280 meters, and causing significant climate changes worldwide. The following year, 1816, known as the year without a summer, saw snow in June and icy rivers in July across Britain, Western Europe, Canada and America.

The occupations of Peterborough folk and the surrounding Fen folk involved dairying, haymaking, planting and harvesting, plus managing livestock such as cattle and sheep that grazed on the rich fertile soil. In winter, they earned a living through fishing and fowling. Crops like wheat, barley and oats were harvested in the spring and summer and held significant value. During the winter, valuable resources included fish, particularly eels, wild birds, peat for fuel and sedge and reed for thatching.

The climate disruption led to crop failures, major food shortages and high prices. In Peterborough, surrounded by the fertile Fens, communities suffered from hunger and disease, with illnesses like typhus spreading.

The substantial release of volcanic ash and gases from Mount Tambora into the atmosphere obstructed sunlight, resulting in global cooling. People experienced significant hardships, including food riots and widespread famine. The situation was further aggravated by the ongoing war with Napoleon, who was considered our national enemy, thereby increasing socio-economic stress.

French prisoners of war were brought to a camp at Norman Cross, Peterborough, via the River Nene. By 1816, the camp housed 10,000 prisoners who sold model ships and other objects made from meat bones and straw at a stall located at the east gate of the camp.

In 1897, Peterborough Natural History, Scientific and Archaeological Society commemorated the centenary of the foundation of Norman Cross Depot with a temporary exhibition in the cathedral precincts. Mr Dack, the museum curator, issued an appeal requesting individuals to search their attics for forgotten family heirlooms – specifically Norman Cross products that may have been acquired by their ancestors. Numerous items were submitted as a result. The discoveries were subsequently displayed in the exhibition and, following its conclusion, most lenders chose to donate their treasures to the society, which later became Peterborough Museum, rather than reclaim them.

Peterborough Museum has an exceptional collection of over 800 Napoleonic prisoner-of-war artefacts. The prisoners created these items to pass time and sell to locals using their skills and expertise. The collection includes decorative and personal items, working models like machines, miniature ships and guillotines familiar to the prisoners.

By 1817, normal weather patterns returned, giving the local population relief.

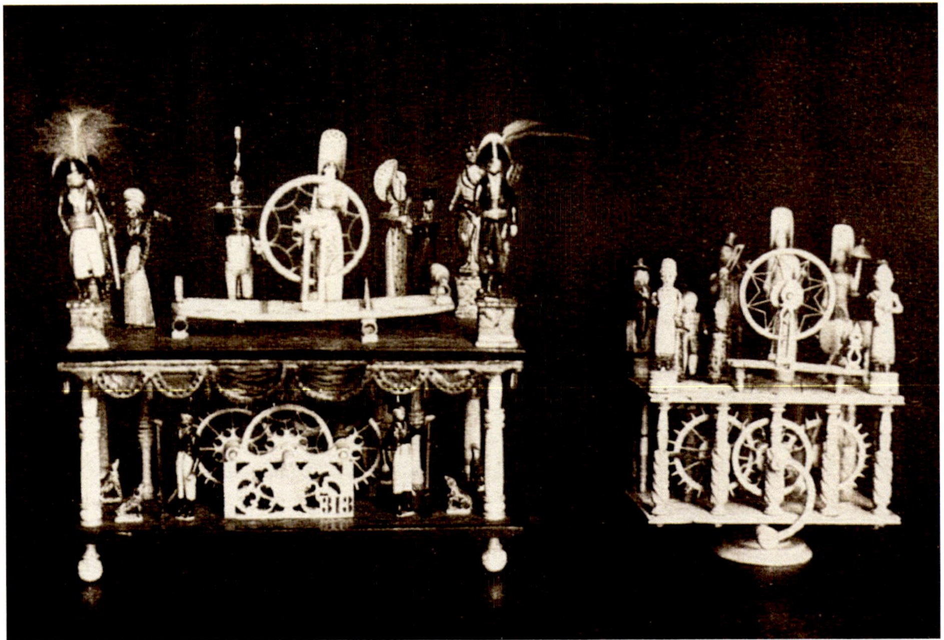

Postcard dated 1947 of Napoleonic POW work from Norman Cross.

Who Is the Real Architect of Thorpe Hall?

Thorpe Hall in Longthorpe, Peterborough, once thought to be designed by John Webb, was identified in the 1950s by researcher Mr Colvin as the work of Peter Mills, a London surveyor. Mills also designed the Hitcham Building at Pembroke College 1659–61, helped design triumphal arches for King Charles II's coronation in 1661, remodelled Cobham Hall's Cross Wing (1661–63) and was appointed as one of the surveyors to rebuild London after the Great Fire of 1666.

In 1850, Revd William Strong of Longthorpe Tower purchased the Thorpe Hall estate in Longthorpe, Peterborough, from Earl Fitzwilliam of neighbouring Milton Hall. At the time, the three-storey stone house was in a state of disrepair. Strong's renovations in the Italian style did not remove its original Cromwellian mansion design by Peter Mills. The latter's final design included contributions from John Stone, a French-trained son of Nicholas Stone. In 1926, the panelled interior of the Great Parlour, attributed to Mills, was transferred to a drawing room at Leeds Castle for Olive, Lady Baillie.

The building dates to Oliver St John (1598–1673), a Lord Chief Justice who supported Parliament in the Civil War and acquired the freehold on an area of Longthorpe – approximately 26 hectares – in 1653. Oliver St John commissioned the construction of Thorpe Hall from 1650 onwards using remnants from Peterborough Cathedral's Bishop's Palace and cloister, as well as stone from Barnack quarries. Thorpe Hall was built between 1653 and 1656.

Mills employed various types of marble along with local stone in his design for Thorpe Hall. The carpentry features scrolls on the architraves and five-panelled oak doors with swags and scrolls. Although the dining room is less than 20 square feet, it includes moulded fruit swags on the ceiling, oak wall panels and doors.

The Grade I listed house is situated within 5 to 6 acres of gardens and outbuildings, enclosed by an ashlar wall. In the mid-nineteenth century, Revd William Strong expanded the walled garden to the west to create a large kitchen garden and added two new lodges. There were two entrance courts: one by road to the north and the other a water access to the south from the River Nene. Pairs of lead falcons adorned both sets of gates.

Upon the death of Revd William Strong, the seat of Thorpe Hall passed to his eldest son, Lieutenant Colonel Charles Isham Strong (1838–1914). After Charles' death, his eldest son Brigadier-General Strong managed Thorpe Hall from 1914 until 1927 when it was acquired by the Meaker family. They undertook modifications to the gardens and replaced many of the rose beds and other garden plants and shrubs.

The Grade II listed gardens were fully restored in 1989, retaining old urns and gates, though most planting dates from post-1990. From 1943 to 1970, Thorpe Hall served as a maternity hospital. In 1986, the Sue Ryder Foundation acquired the property, opening it as a hospice in May 1991 where it remains operational.

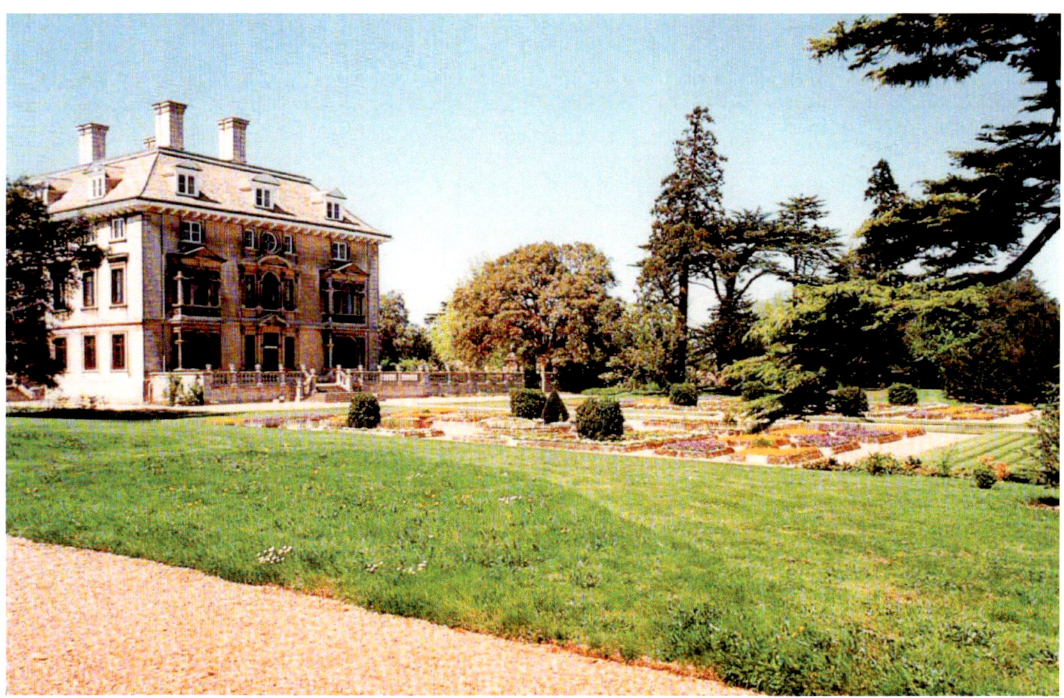

Thorpe Hall in 1988.

In November 2011, the Sue Ryder Foundation received planning permission from Peterborough City Council and English Heritage to construct a new single-storey hospice within the existing grounds. The facility offers twenty single en-suite bedrooms within a landscaped garden, fully accessible to patients and relatives. It is available for wedding hire and the gardens are accessible to the public throughout the year.

Lord Orford's Voyage

In the late eighteenth century, Lord Orford, the Rt Hon. George Walpole, Lord of the Bedchamber to King George III, and his fellow sailors visited Peterborough. Instead of touring Europe on a grand tour, they explored the Fens, starting on 16 July 1774. They travelled in a fleet of nine barges called fenlighters, pulled by a large horse named 'Hippopotamus' ('river horse' in Greek).

Accompanying him on his voyage of the Fens was his mistress, Martha Turk, and various influential friends, some of whom joined him in keeping a record of events. His route on the River Nene took in Outwell, March, Whittlesey Mere, Peterborough, Benwick and then back up the River Ouse to Lakenheath, Suffolk. These part-time mariners did find plenty to praise, but they also made some pompous and scathing remarks concerning the appearance of folk and their environment.

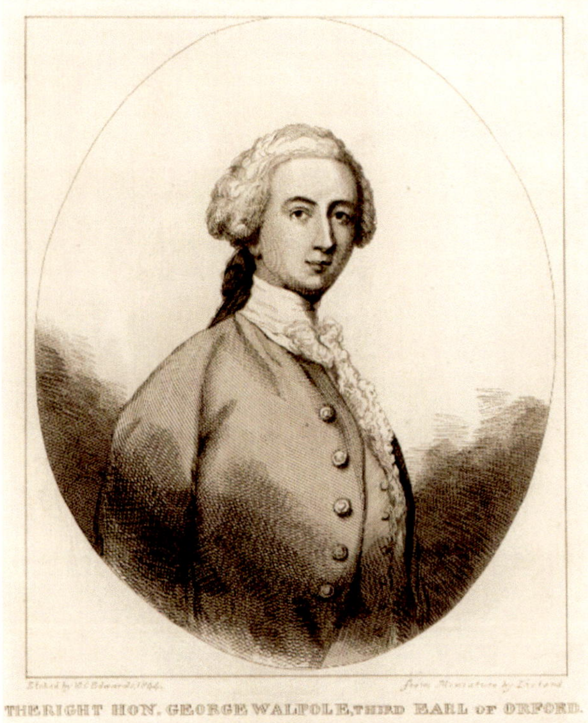

Lord of the Bedchamber to King George III.

From 20 to 21 July, they moored beside the Town Bridge in Peterborough, with views of the cathedral and Bishop's Palace, the latter Orford reported as unimpressive. They stayed in Farcet Bay while one of their fenlighters, *The Centaurus*, got a new mast but not a sail due to distractions from the local by-election. However, they acquired two haunches of venison and some Stilton cheese that evening. The fenlighter, one of nine, was fully repaired a day later.

On 29 July, Orford and his men dined with the Bishop of Peterborough and toured the palace gardens. That evening, Mr Roberts, a fellow sailor of Lord Orford, injured his shin assisting a lady at Peterborough's playhouse (located where St John's Square is today), marking the fleet's only casualty. On 30 July, the fleet left Peterborough via Stanground and halted at Horsey Bridge to explore Civil War fortifications. The voyage took twenty-two days, ending on 6 August 1774.

Lord Orford's real passions were hunting and hare coursing; he was also a celebrated falconer, but was also known for being extravagantly reckless. He became increasingly eccentric and died in 1791, aged sixty-one, mentally unwell and without heirs, so the title passed to his uncle, Horace Walpole.

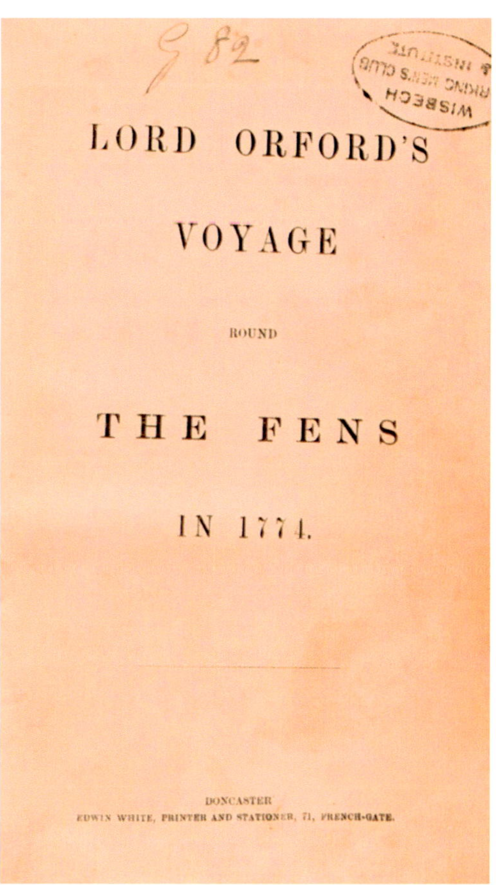

Inside cover of a book published in 1868.

Paston Hall Museum

Before Paston Hall (constructed around 1618) was demolished, it experienced two significant fires. The first occurred around 1800 and the second took place in 1870, when it was rebuilt in a more modern style.

In the 1930s, Frederick Charles Ihlee, an engineer by trade, rented the hall. He was renowned for his collection of English eighteenth- and nineteenth-century model warships. He was born in Britain in 1868 to German parents who had left Germany in *c.* 1863. In his later years, he was the Managing Director of Werner, Pfleiderer and Perkins Ltd, located on Westfield Road in Peterborough (the company later became Baker Perkins), from 1915 until his death in 1938. Frederick began buying and repairing model warships in 1924 because he worried they were being sold to the American market.

His extensive collection, which included some unique items, was housed in a wing of Paston Hall that was specifically designed as a museum for public viewing. HMS *Queen*, 1839, was a notable piece in the collection as it was not a dockyard model but a rigger's model made to a scale of 1 in 120. Frederick personally restored its rigging. His collection included three models of Nelson's HMS *Victory* from 1765. He donated his extensive collection, many of which were meticulously restored, to the Science Museum.

The hall was demolished in 1958 after the Co-op stopped using it as a social club.

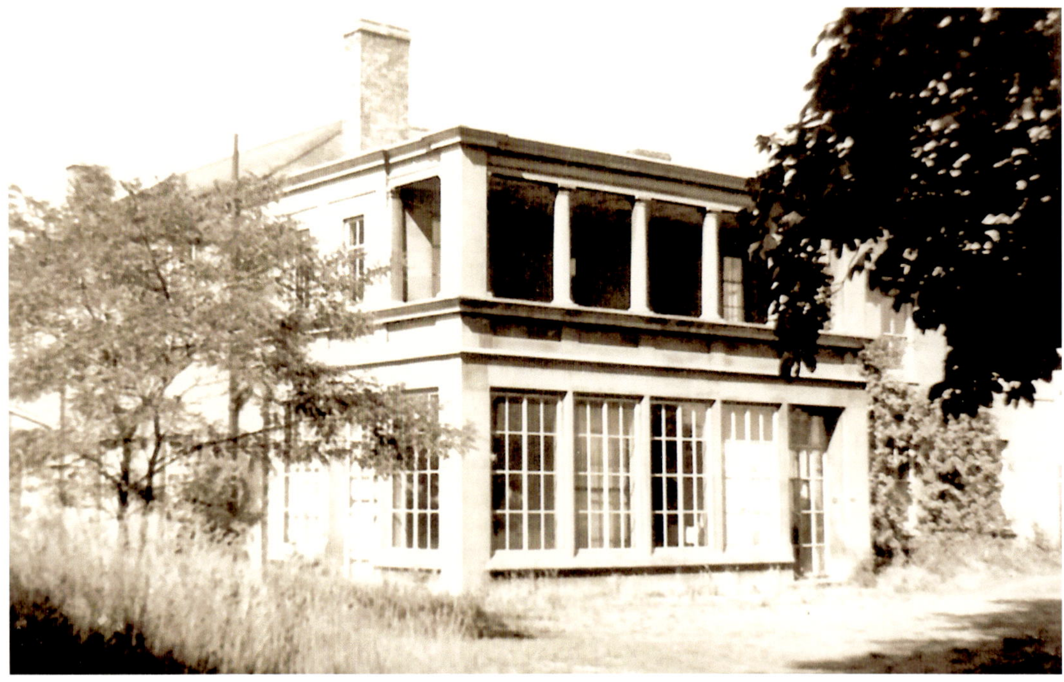

Paston Hall, *c.* 1955.

Two Farewells to the Comet

The first record traced to the Comet Beer House on Garton Road is from 1846 when an inquest into the death of William Plant was held there. Where the name Comet came from is unclear, but it could be a reference to Haley's Comet, which appeared on 16 November 1835, then 20 April 1910, 9 February 1986 and is due again on 28 July 2061.

Next, we find a *Stamford Mercury* newspaper article published on 9 June 1882 relating to the Comet Beer House. A certain Alfred Bentick went in to pay his debt and passed a foreign coin as payment, pretending it was a sovereign. He was promptly arrested by the police and a month later brought before the court, where a judge and jury found him guilty and sentenced him to six months' hard labour. Reporters present said that Bendick gave the warders a great deal of trouble as he was led away to be taken to prison.

The Comet Beer House served the local community well and in 1899 the annual meeting of the Garton End Pig Club was held there each September.

In 1924, the beer house was pulled down and a new pub of the same name was erected, with a full licence being granted in 1935. In the 1990s the pub changed its name to the Elm Tree Tavern and then reverted to its original name of the Comet in *c.* 2004. The brewery, Admiral Taverns, deemed the pub unviable and it finally closed its doors in December 2022.

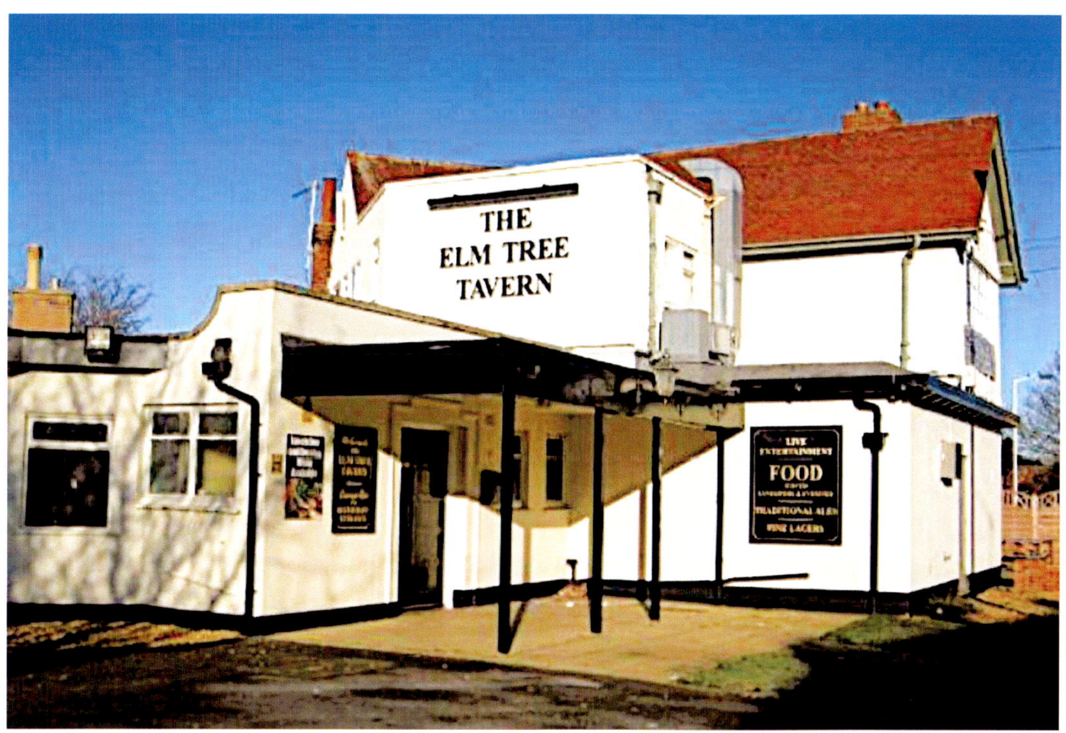

Elm Tree Tavern, *c.* 2000.

The following summer, Peterborough City Council's Planning Department received an application from its new owners for the demolition and erection of seven new three-bed houses on the site. The application was granted unanimously by the planning committee.

Great Bands

The Beatles, later referred to as 'the Fab Four', played their first show outside of Liverpool at Peterborough's Embassy Theatre on 2 December 1962 and returned on 17 March 1963, staying at the Bull Hotel. Many notable groups have performed in our city since then. Several famous bands have performed in Peterborough during their peak years, including prominent 1960s groups such as The Who, The Kinks, The Animals and The Hollies, as well as bands from the 1970s like The Sweet, Bay City Rollers, Genesis and Roxy Music. Additionally, punk groups such as The Clash, Buzzcocks and The Damned have also played here.

The Rolling Stones turned up tired and hungry for an early gig at the Corn Exchange, Church Street. Before fame struck, unknowns like Queen, Mott The Hoople, Thin Lizzy, Status Quo, Black Sabbath, Radiohead, Keane and Kasabian all played here.

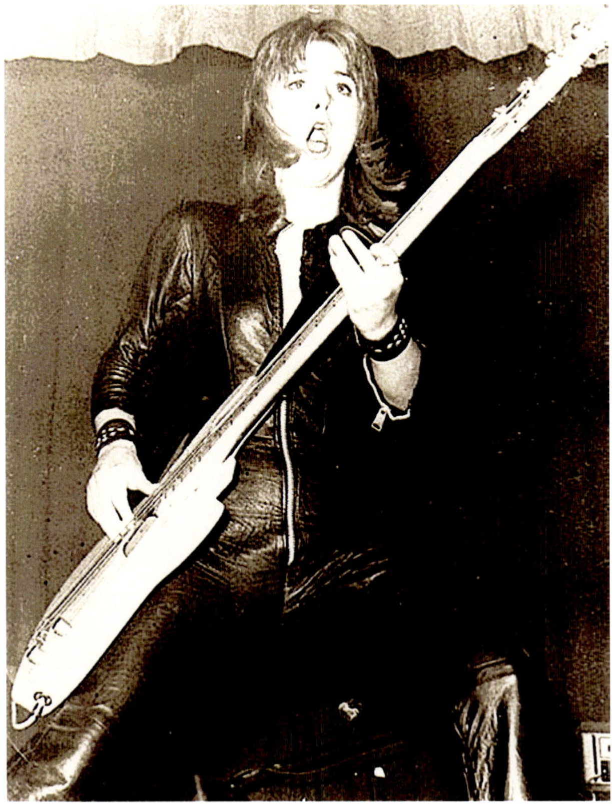

Suzi Quatro at the Wirrina in 1974. (Photo courtesy of Ian Southerland)

Early debuts in some of our pubs included Jon Lord of Deep Purple, Rick Wakeman of Yes, Richie Blackmore of Deep Purple, plus Christine McVie of Fleetwood Mac and very many more.

The Searchers performed at the Palais on Wentworth Street twice: the first time on 23 January 1965 and the second time on 8 January 1966. The Small Faces also held a performance at the Palais on 14 May 1966. Additionally, The Sex Pistols played outside the Guildhall in the city centre on Christmas Eve 1977.

Slade performed at the Wirrina Stadium on 19 January 1981, where artists like Elvis Costello and Suzi Quatro also played. Some prominent venues included Cloud Nine, the Cresset, the East of England Showground, St John's Hall and Peterborough Technical College. Additionally, various nightclubs attracted many famous and emerging bands due to the city's good road connections.

In 1989, the rock band Queen filmed a video at the Nene Valley Railway for their single 'Breakthru', which reached No. 7 in the UK charts.

The Rudest Man in the Church of England

Douglas Feaver served as the Bishop of Peterborough from 1972 to 1984. He held strong and well-established views on various matters, including his opposition to women in the priesthood, and consistently expressed these views during his tenure.

He was intimidating, often dismantling weak arguments at bishops' meetings with his sharp mind and biting tongue. However, he welcomed those who challenged him and enjoyed engaging in debates.

Canon John Howitt, Vicar and Rural Dean of Peterborough, often observed that Bishop Douglas was kind, warm and humorous beneath his exterior. Mrs Howitt once joked about the bishop wearing a dress, which led to mutual respect. Barbara Howitt later became a vicar after the death of her husband.

While at Keble College, Oxford, Douglas Feaver earned a double first in History and Theology. He then spent twenty years at St Albans Cathedral, first as a curate and later as a canon and sub-dean. His theological career was only interrupted by the Second World War, when he served as a chaplain in the Royal Air Force Volunteer Reserve. It was during this time he became seriously ill in Egypt; while he was lying in his sickbed, he heard his grave being dug in front of the hospital, but he recovered. After the war, he became the vicar of St Mary's Church, Nottingham. This appointment led to his subsequent appointment as the Bishop of Peterborough.

He described the Peterborough diocese as one of the best in England and mentioned that he found his job very satisfactory. Familiar with both rural and urban areas, Bishop Douglas did not see the necessity for a suffragan bishop and preferred traditional practices, such as using the Book of Common Prayer when he conducted public worship. Bishop Douglas's pastoral work was acknowledged by many, including the Duke of Gloucester and his family, who at

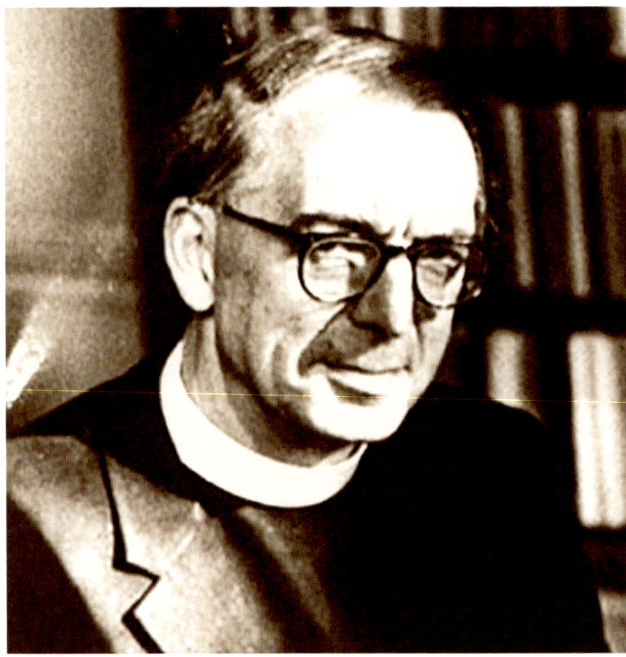

Revd Douglas Feaver.
(Courtesy of St Mary
the Virgin Church,
Nottingham, *c.* 1942)

the time resided in the diocese, at Barnwell Manor. He took a special interest in
the younger clergy to ensure that they did some solid theological reading.

Bishop Douglas had two wives. He had three children with his first wife and
remarried after her death in 1987. Both marriages were harmonious as each wife
was a great match for him.

Countless anecdotes and sayings of Bishop Douglas have been handed down:

- Nothing is so tedious and ephemeral as the neurotic lust for novelty.
- Virtuous women abound in Rutland.
- There are three women in my life: my mother, my wife and Our Lady.
- One line of poetry is nearer to the heart of mystery than ten thousand words
  of trite explanation.
- I believe that Christians ought to learn again the art of asking awkward
  questions.
- He is reported to have said of a fellow member of the House of Lords: His
  mouth is for export only. His head has no entrance.

Poverty, Misery and Hopelessness

In 1834, the Poor Law Union replaced the Elizabethan system. During the
Victorian period, there was a belief that the poor should help themselves. Parishes
were grouped to share workhouses, providing accommodation and work. The
'idle poor', as they were termed, were seen as responsible for their situation and
had to work to improve it.

It was up to people who needed help to apply for admission and then to leave the workhouse when they had work. Conditions discouraged inmates from staying as they were deliberately less comfortable than the average workers' accommodation.

The Poor Law Union Workhouses in Peterborough were overseen by a local Board of Guardians, established in 1835. A new workhouse was built on Thorpe Road, managed by a master and his wife, who served as matron. The staff included a porter and eventually two teachers for the children. Additional buildings such as a hospital and chapel were later added.

Once their food allocation was decided, each person's diet number was attached to their clothes. Families were separated, with men and women kept in different parts of the building and children taken away from their parents upon entering the workhouse. Children were supposed to receive some form of education.

Most men recorded their regular occupation as agricultural workers. Individuals entered the workhouse for various reasons, including destitution, old age, infirmity, blindness, mental illness, infancy, paralysis, seizures, abandonment or being unmarried girls without accommodation. Records show that some older boys secured apprenticeships while older girls generally entered domestic service.

People living in poverty faced significant challenges in meeting their own basic needs, such as food and clothing. Those who were physically or mentally disabled

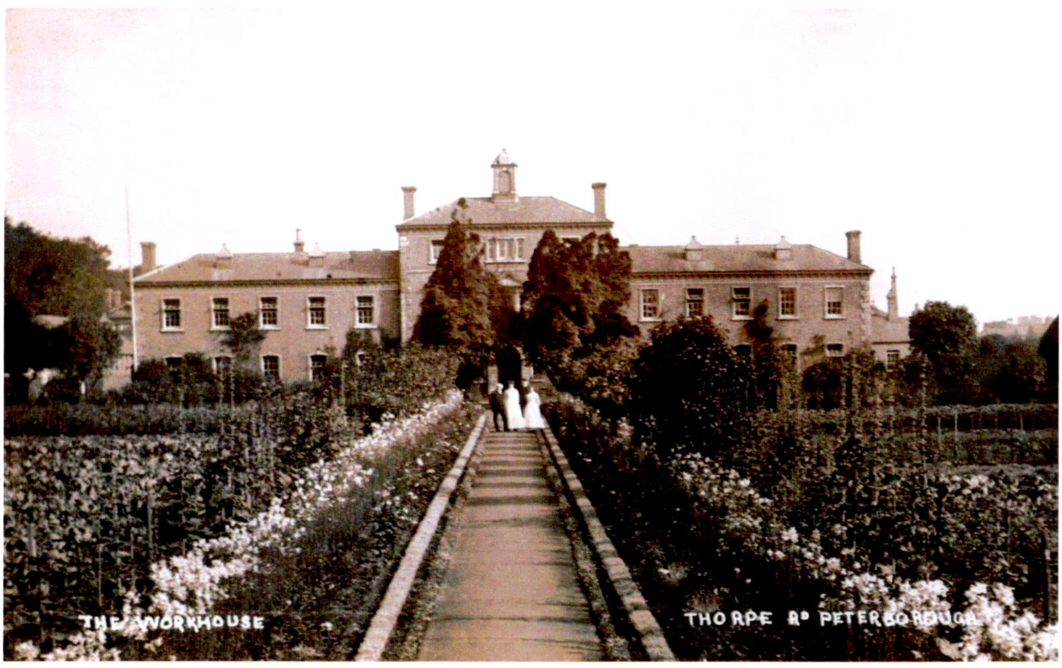

The workhouse, *c.* 1904.

often found themselves in workhouses, where they were unlikely to find work or become self-supporting.

Thankfully, the National Health Service was established in 1948. Social security benefits, based primarily on the contributory principle, were introduced in the first half of the twentieth century. As a result, workhouses started to decline; the one on Thrope Road was demolished in 1971.

The Poltergeist of Mayor's Walk

The Peterborough Advertiser published an article about an unusual event in its edition dated 9 January 1892. The story concerned the Rimes family, residing at No. 22 Mayor's Walk, although due to renumbering, current occupants are unaware of this history. The family moved there when Mr Rimes accepted a position with the Midland Railway. The household included Mr and Mrs Rimes; their three sons; Mrs Rimes' brother, Mr Want; and her brother-in-law, Mr Easy. Mr Easy also worked for the Midland Railway. The property had three bedrooms and an upstairs landing. The front bedroom was occupied by Mr Want and one of the boys; the second bedroom by Mr Easy and the other two boys; and the back bedroom by Mr and Mrs Rimes.

Shortly after moving in, the family was disturbed by nightly knocks at the door, but no one was there upon answering. Assuming it was children playing pranks, they ignored it. In early November 1892, an unnatural wind blew through the house, removing bed covers. They first thought it was a weather anomaly but

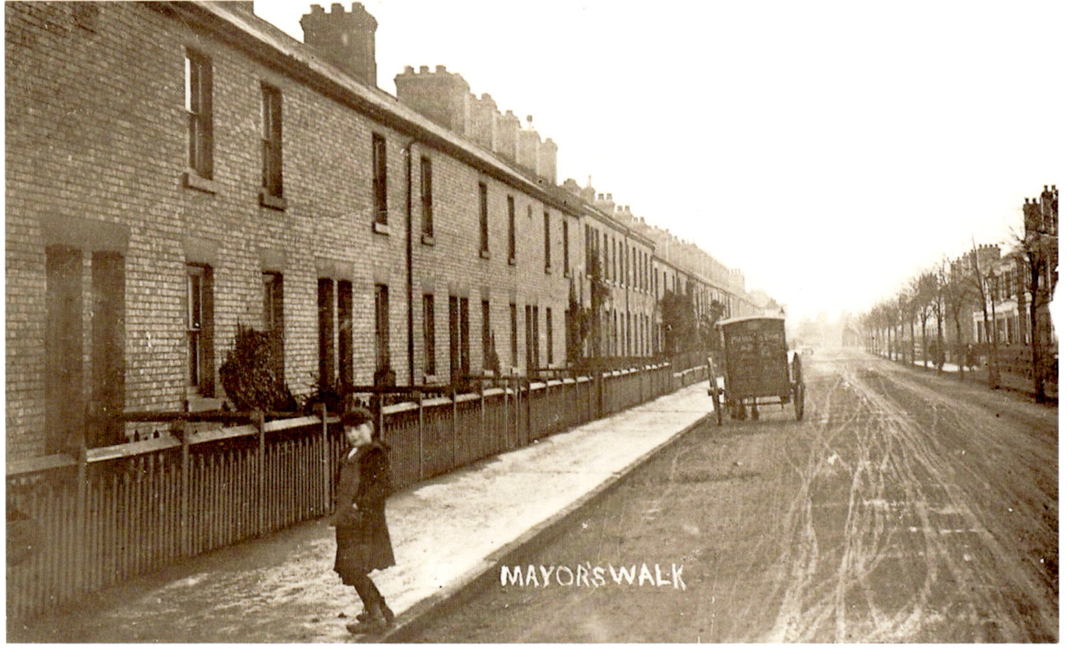

Mayor's Walk, *c.* 1908.

soon experienced nightly knocking, tapping, and banging from the landing. These noises increased in intensity, shaking doors and walls, even to the point of breaking a handle off a door.

After a week of disturbances, Mrs Rimes' brother, Mr Want, moved his bed to keep watch but saw nothing causing the noises. Despite the occupants removing wall panels and floorboards, no explanation was found. The sounds grew so loud that by Christmas even neighbours were disturbed. On 29 December, the banging substantially intensified, prompting the family to huddle in the kitchen until dawn. Shortly after, the Rimes family and their lodgers moved to Monument Street.

It is said that poltergeists, or noisy spirits, haunt people rather than property and can be connected to their troubled past.

Two Katherine Claytons

Katherine Emily was born in Leicester. Her father was Thomas Hare, born in 1803, a Liberal reformer and barrister by profession. He held the position of inspector of charities and set out a proposal to use proportional representation to elect MPs to Parliament in 1859. This policy was backed by economists like John Mills and Henry Fawcett. Later, Thomas became involved in the call for women's suffrage, speaking at public meetings and joining campaign groups. It is then little wonder that his daughter, Katherine Emily, became involved in women's suffrage, joining the debating society and the Kensington Society, who often discussed the matter. Katherine also signed various petitions to Parliament from 1866 onwards.

In 1872, Katherine Emily Hare married Dr Lewis Clayton, who would become Assistant Bishop of Peterborough. The couple moved to Peterborough, where they brought up their four children. Katherine Emily continued her involvement in the campaign for votes for women, signing a memorandum to Sir Arthur Balfour in 1896 asking the government to give time to discuss the matter in Parliament.

Katherine also attended local meetings for women's suffrage with her daughter, Katherine, known as Kitty. Both attended a meeting with Emmeline Pankhurst at the Fitzwilliam Rooms of the Angel Hotel on 11 February 1911.

Katherine Clayton, née Hare, was also involved in campaigns concerning education and she was awarded an OBE for her work. She was made freeman of Peterborough for her social work. One of Katherine's local campaigns was raising money to replace the marble tomb of Katherine of Aragon at Peterborough Cathedral, as a former bishop had broken up the former memorial to use for his conservatory.

Katherine, known as Kitty, was born in 1877. Her father, Dr Lewis Clayton, was not only Assistant Bishop of Peterborough but later Suffragan Bishop of Leicester, and as above her mother Katherine Emily was highly active in social, scholastic and political reforms.

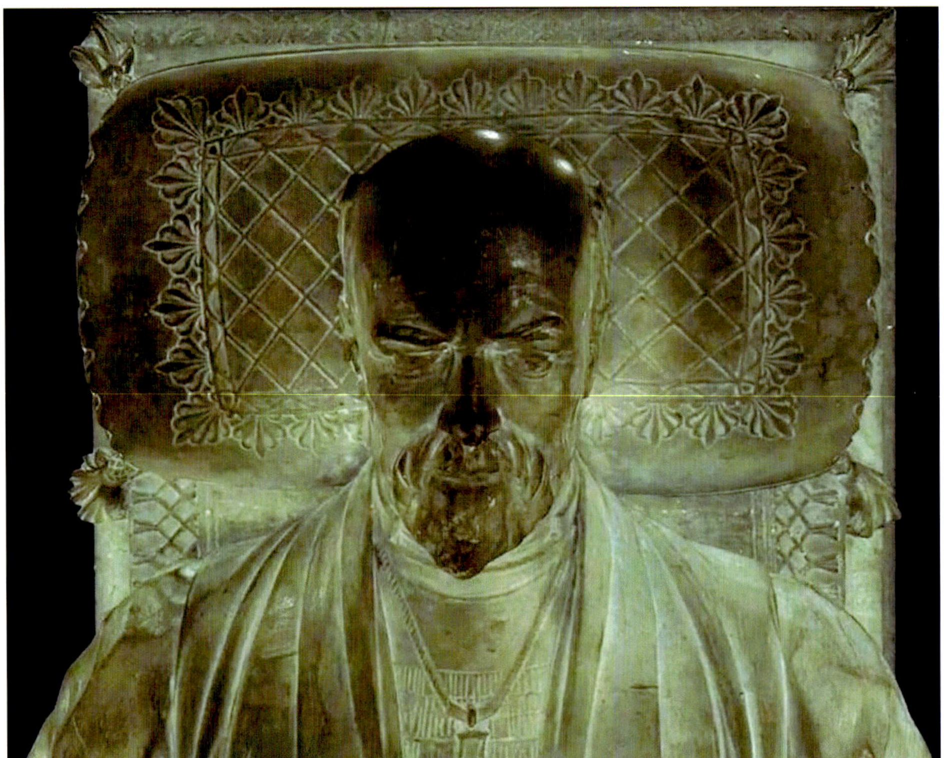

Dr Lewis Clayton, Assistant Bishop of Peterborough.

On 17 January 1901, Kitty married Revd Robert Edwin Roberts, who was born in Wales, served as a master at the Choir School of Westminster Abbey, saw active service in the First World War as a chaplain, worked in a munitions factory and later became a canon and dean of Leicester Cathedral. Reportedly a gifted baritone singer who gave lectures in Welsh, Irish and Scottish music, Robert Roberts also compiled hymnals and composed the tune 'Philippine', named after his daughter, born in 1919.

Kitty and Robert wrote a history of Peterborough that was published in 1920 in the series *The Story of English Towns*. Kitty translated and paraphrased Welsh carols for *The Oxford Book of Carols*. She also wrote the baptism text for her husband's tune, 'Philippine'.

Like mother, like daughter. Our city had two pioneering women who advocated for better education, social integration and political reform. Katherine Clayton died in 1933 and her daughter Kitty in 1962.

It is of note that Emeline Pankhurst, founder of the British suffragette movement, previously visited Peterborough on 22 February 1910, where she spoke about women's emancipation at a public meeting held at the Corn Exchange in Church Street.

City Centre Fires

In the sixteenth and seventeenth centuries two major fires burnt out large areas of wooden houses in Westgate and Bridge Street, with the only means of extinguishing them being hand pumps operated by volunteers who were paid in beer. For one man the temptation of free beer was too much; he set about starting fires deliberately in expectation of free drink, but was found out and hanged.

In 1834, over thirty houses in Westgate were destroyed by fire, with the loss of one life. A decade later an official fire service was set up, but they had no access to a good, pumped water supply. Thus, they were ill equipped to deal with the infirmary fire in Priestgate, now the museum, when fire broke out in 1884. While there was no loss of life, it did highlight the need for more effective measures in the future. To this end, a group of local businessmen met at the Angel Hotel to discuss the way forward and Peterborough Volunteer Fire Service was formed as a result. The latter are still in action today and the only one operating of its kind. In 1984, they were awarded the freedom of the city. Peterborough Volunteer Fire Services attended the fire that broke out at the Phoenix Brewery in Priestgate, which coincidently was opposite the infirmary.

In the mid-twentieth century, a passer-by spotted a fire in the window of Robert Sayle's department store in Cowgate, with flames reaching well over 100 ft high engulfing the four-storey building and spreading to other nearby premises. Over 100 firemen attended, but they were unable to stop the destruction. Two firefighters were taken to hospital and treated for burns and smoke inhalation; otherwise, there were no casualties.

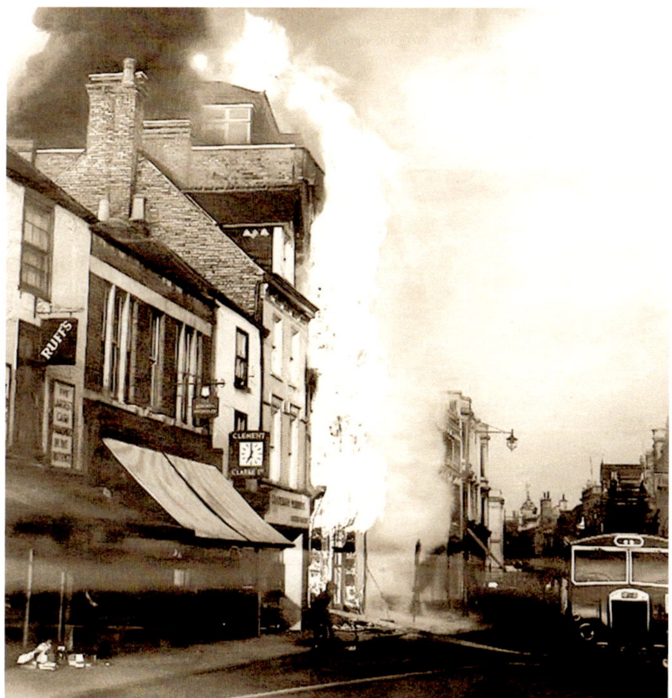

Robert Sayle's shop on fire in 1956.

Peterborough Abbey had suffered at least two earlier fires in its long history, but on 22 November 2001 the cathedral could have completely burnt down had it not been for the verger walking through the minster precinct that evening and noticing a flickering light through the windows. The alarm was raised; it was feared that the wooden vaulted ceiling might be destroyed or the roof collapse. Thankfully a greater disaster was averted by the fire brigade and other emergency services attending so swiftly. The fire was lit under a stack of plastic chairs, but the arsonist was never caught. The cleaning and conservation work of the organ-cracked windows and vaulted ceiling, the oldest and largest painted wooden ceiling in Europe, took five years at a cost of £1.25 million.

Peterborough Youth Council

The Youth Council in Peterborough consists of young people aged eleven to eighteen who meet monthly to represent their peers. Two members from each secondary school or college bring forward views, promote activities and engage with local and national governments. They form working groups on issues like underrepresentation and report back to the full council. Additionally, they participate in the British Youth Council and UK Youth Parliament. Peterborough currently has two Youth MPs serving two-year terms.

Being on the Youth Council involves campaigning on issues important to young people and assisting Peterborough City Council and local organisations to ensure young people are given the opportunity to have a say on the decisions that most affect them.

The above is particularly important given that the 2021 census data shows that our city has a high proportion of younger people compared to older individuals.

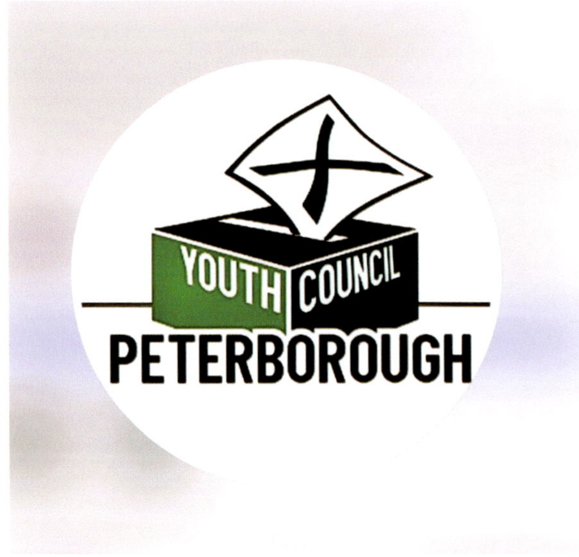

Peterborough Youth Council's voting logo.

This demographic trend is one that some cities most seek, as young people contribute and drive future economic prosperity and growth.

Peterborough Youth Council also recognises the remarkable work of young people through the Bright Futures Awards for those aged eleven to eighteen, academic years 7–13, under six categories, namely Science, Technology, Engineering and Mathematics; Humanities; Visual Arts; Performing Arts; Sports; and Social Action. This is so that students' achievements are recognised within all fields whether they aspire to become engineers, doctors or actors. Each category is split into age groups so that young people across the age ranges can be rewarded for their work. The awards are promoted and sponsored by local organisations and businesses.

Warship Week

Warship weeks were British National Savings campaigns during the Second World War, with a Royal Navy warship being adopted by communities. The Royal Navy had not only lost many ships at the beginning of the war, but losses continued when navy ships became escorts for convoys in the Atlantic. While there was no shortage of sailors, many ships were sunk by enemy action and needed to be replaced. The British Army had an equivalent campaign called Salute the Soldier Week and the Royal Airforce had Wings for Victory Week.

Our city stepped up to the plate; there were 574 savings groups in the city by September 1941. At a meeting of Peterborough Local Savings Committee, it was proposed to buy a destroyer in Warship Week at a cost of £450,000, but the cost increased to £700,000. As a submarine could be bought for £425,000, it was decided that this would be the new aim.

Warship Week essentially covered a period of ten days from 27 November and ended on 6 December 1941. Originally, the committee had settled on the destroyer named HMS *Peterborough*, but the submarine HMS *Olympus* was to be adopted by the city.

Donations large and small came from all over the city: shops, schools, societies and individual citizens. At the end of Warship Week, a grand total of £523,000 was reached, being £98,000 over the original target, with £109,000 of the total coming from banks and individual savings accounts.

A heavy bronze plaque was fixed inside the submarine HMS *Olympus* which read: 'To commemorate the adoption of HMS Olympus by the citizens of Peterborough and District – Peterborough Warship Week, Nov 27th – Dec 6th, 1941.'

At the end of May 1941, our city received the shield from the Admiralty bearing the crest of HMS *Olympus* and commemorating the money it had raised to buy the adopted submarine. Little did they know at the time, however, that the submarine had already been sunk off Malta on 8 May 1942.

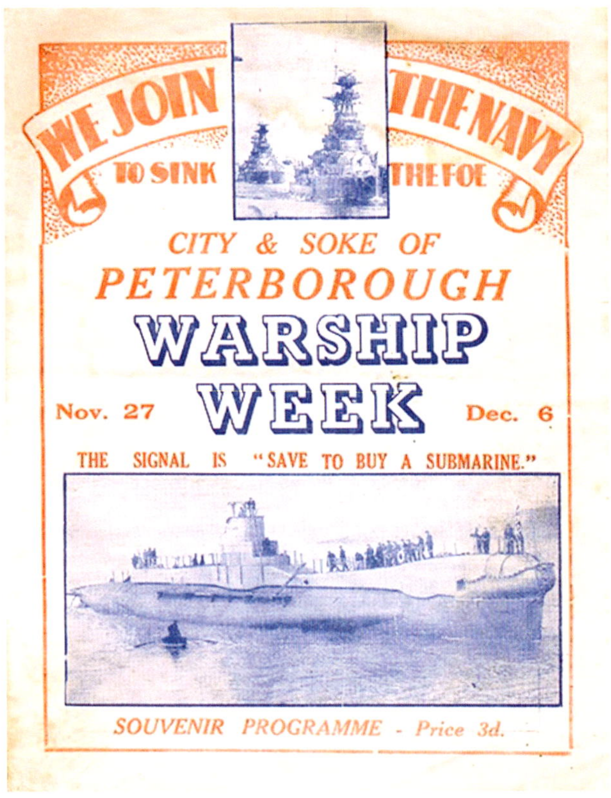

Left: Warship Week leaflet, 1941.

Below: HMS *Olympus*, a Royal Navy submarine, *c*. 1930.

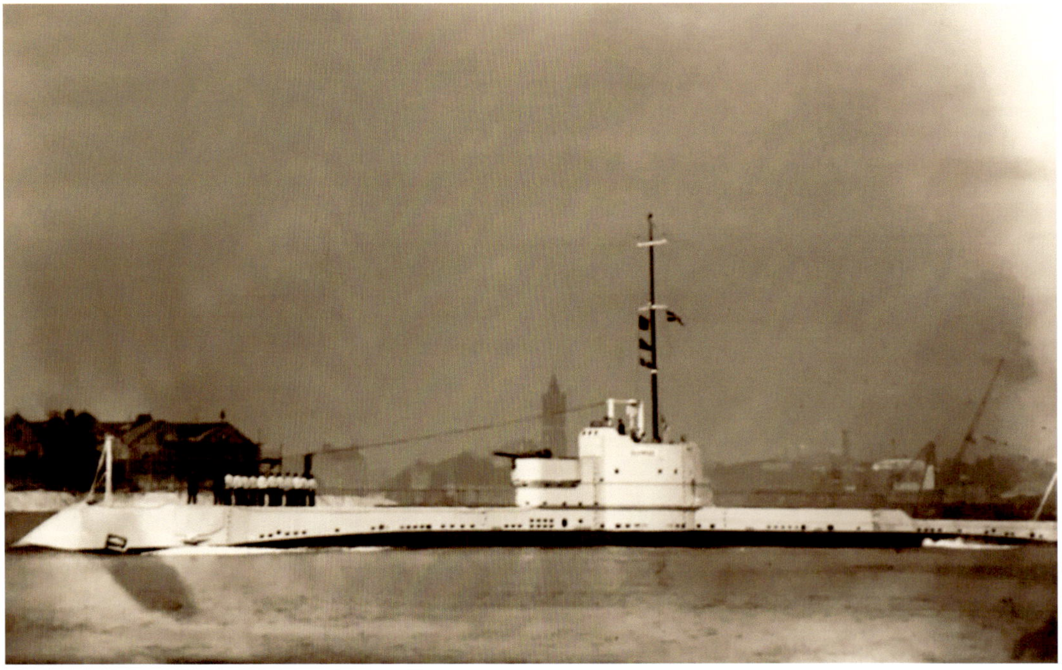

It didn't take long for the Admiralty to find a replacement submarine, and on 25 June 1942 the city's savings group were told that they had been allocated the submarine HMS *P512* to replace HMS *Olympus*. This vessel survived the war and was sold for scrap to the North American Smelting Co., Philadelphia, on 16 November 1945.

Alfred John Paten

Paten came to our city in 1898 and secured a loan from the brewers Bass & Co., founded in 1777, and started trading at age nineteen in Long Causeway. He bought the property and wider business of Alderman Nichols, three times mayor. Included in the deal was The Bull and Dolphin pub, No. 94 Bridge Street, where he also bottled Bass beer. On 17 December 1898, he placed an advertisement in the *Peterborough Advertiser* announcing the new management and pricing. Thus, Patens was launched.

Alfred first lived at the Crescent, demolished in 1913 to make way for the Crescent Railway Bridge. In 1900, he married Emily Stokes from Warmington, and they both settled at Airedale on Dogsthorpe Road. The couple had three children: Henry, known as Harry, Lionel and Joyce. All three children had 'Brading' included in their names in recognition of their paternal grandmother, and each was given £25 – a fairly considerable sum back then.

In just over two decades the family moved house five times. Between 1905 and 1907 they lived in Hunstanton, where their daughter Joyce was born, to save the money needed for A. J. Paten's first company expansion. When Alfred's mother, Emily Brading, died they moved back to the Peterborough area in 1907, living at The Cedars, Castor. Eventually they were able to purchase The Lindens, Lincoln Road, in 1921.

Alfred expanded his business empire by buying public houses in Ramsey, Stamford, Loughborough and Melton Mowbray. He always insisted that tea and coffee be available in all the company's licensed premises.

In 1908 Paten & Co. were approved suppliers of bottled ales and stout to the Great Northern Railway at Grantham, Newark and Spalding. Deliveries were made by horse and dray, with the first lorry being purchased at the end of the First World War.

Paten's premises at No. 19 Long Causeway included offices on the first floor, a shop and a pub named The Black Boy & Trumpet together with bottling facilities and cellars. Paten's also owned The Maltings on Alderman's Drive, advertising themselves as 'wine shippers'. That building was demolished and is now a residential care home retaining the name The Maltings.

All of Alfred's life he was concerned with cleanliness and style and always dressed smartly. He adored elegant cars and owned a Hispano Suiza and a Rolls-Royce among his collection. Alfred enjoyed golf and was a member of Walton Golf Club as well as being a Freemason at Fitzwilliam Lodge, located

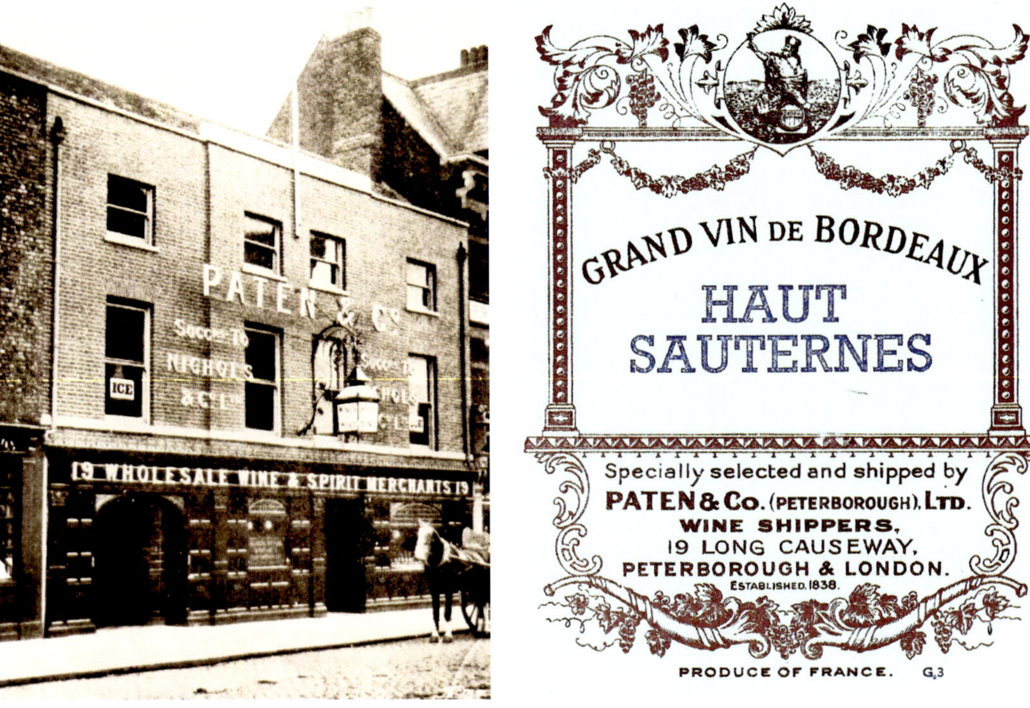

Above left: Black Boy & Trumpet pub, No. 19 Long Causeway, *c.* 1910.

Above right: Paten & Co. wine label for a grand Bordeaux wine.

at Boroughbury, now at Ellindon in Ravensthorpe. It is said he would have a £5 note sewn into the lining of each of his suits so that if he was robbed when he travelled to London on business, he would have enough money for a room at the Savoy and a first-class rail ticket home.

Plane Lands on New Soke Parkway

The first 3 miles of Soke Parkway was under construction when Barry Tempest was forced to land his light plane on the half-finished carriageway in October 1972 due to thick fog, and later he took off after a flurry of media attention.

The construction of the parkway was not without incident, however. On another occasion outside of working hours, a few impulsive teenagers were unable to stop a bulldozer they had deliberately started and it went on to demolish a partly completed footbridge.

However, this prompted, in quick succession, the start of Nene Parkway in March 1972, including Peterborough's long-awaited second river bridge, and in March 1973 the second stretch of Soke Parkway, which followed in part the Crab and Winkle railway line to the north of New England. The affectionately named Crab and Winkle railway line was established in 1866 and ran through Peterborough, Wisbech and Sutton Bridge. It bisected Paston Lane in Peterborough and ran behind where Robert and Bluebell Avenues are today. In 1893, the company amalgamated with the Midland & Great Northern Joint Railway, bringing easier access to the Norfolk coast. The Crab and Winkle line transported day trippers and holidaymakers to Cromer and Great Yarmouth, whilst freight trains supplied our citizens with fresh shellfish until the route's closure on 2 February 1959. Its course can still be traced as a footpath that runs parallel with Soke Parkway.

When completed in February 1975, these roads, together with the first section of Soke Parkway, provided an 8-mile motorway bypass around the west and north of the city centre, freeing it of heavy A15 and A47 through traffic which previously had congested and polluted the main shopping streets.

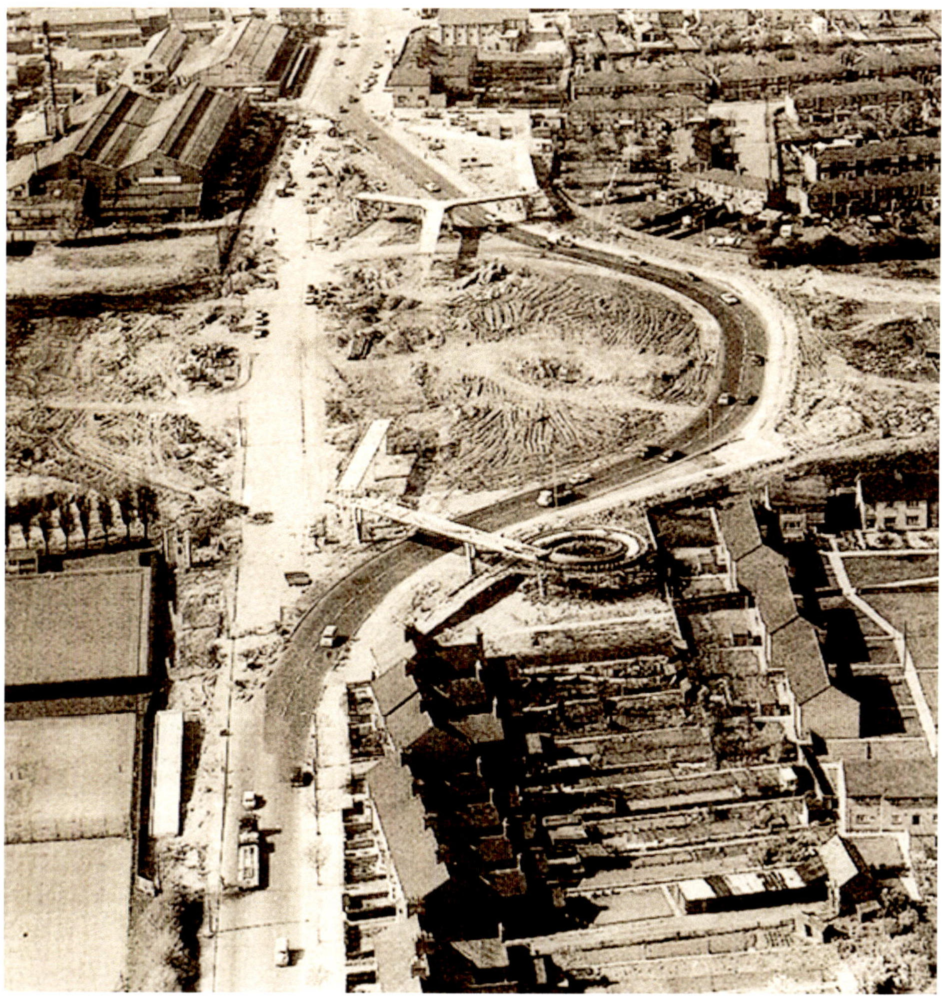

An aerial view of Soke Parkway, Walton, in 1971.

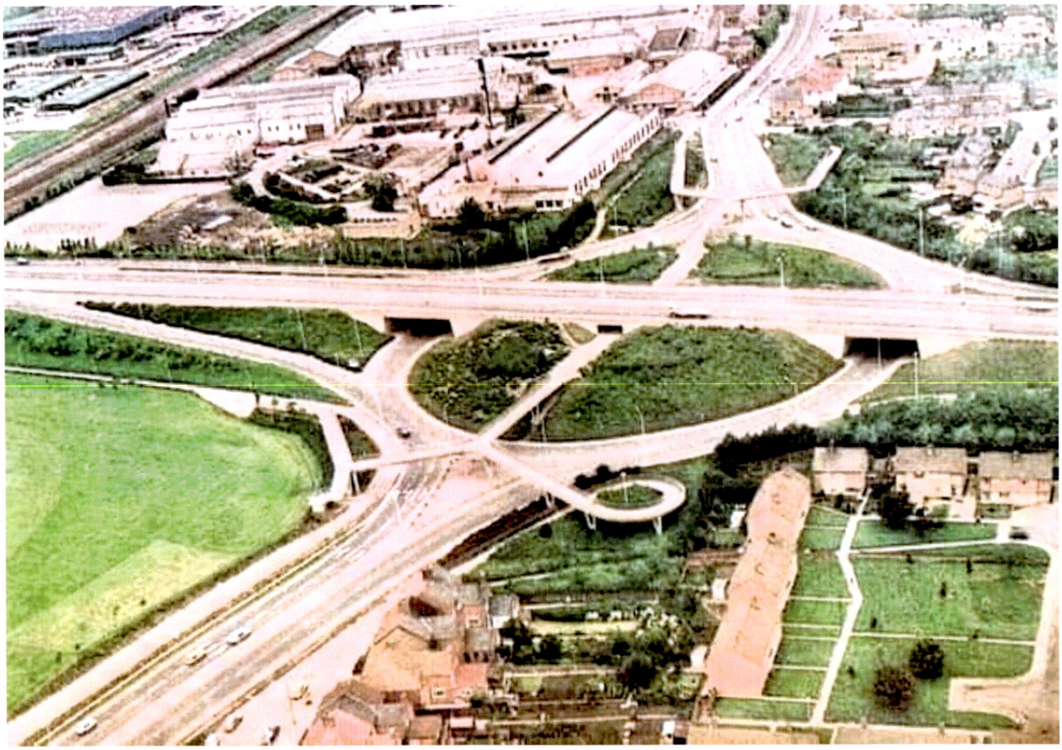

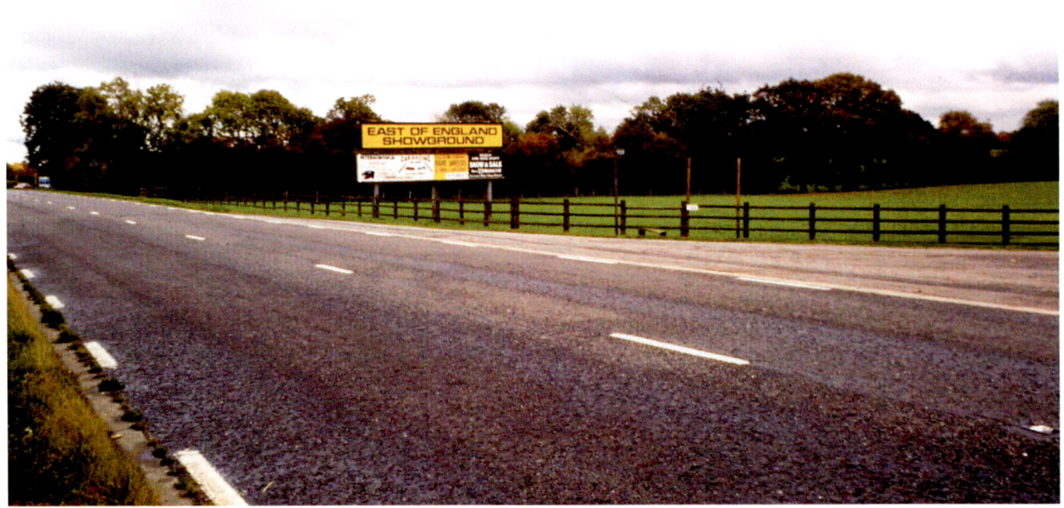

Lincoln Road's Soke Parkway interchange is one of the city's busiest roads, *c.* 1976.

Entrance to the East of England Showground, Alwalton.

Parkway contracts were being let every year during the 1970s. The first stretch of Fletton Parkway was completed in July 1976. Running along the southern boundary of the government's New Town's designated area, it linked Nene Parkway to the A1 and with the first section of Orton Parkway, built under the same contract, gave access for opening up the Orton Township.

Apart from providing an alternative east–west through route, Fletton Parkway put the East of England Showground on the map, making it potentially the most accessible showground in the country.

The opening of the first stretch of Frank Perkins Parkway by the Secretary of State, Nicholas Ridley, took place on 4 December 1984, enabling even more traffic to keep flowing round the city.

The Great Drought of 1868

George Gaunt, who resided in Broadway, owned farmland in Eastfield and had a butcher's shop in Westgate, had the only pump in the city that did not run dry during the drought of 1868. At that time, Frog Hall Lane, now Princes Gardens, had no houses, New Road had very few, and there were none between Eastfield and New England. It was mainly ploughed fields.

The drought of 1868 started early and lasted through May, June and July. The first pump to run dry was the town pump in Cumbergate, followed by another in Long Causeway. The pump outside St John's Church withstood the draught and was the last to dry out after supplying the town with water.

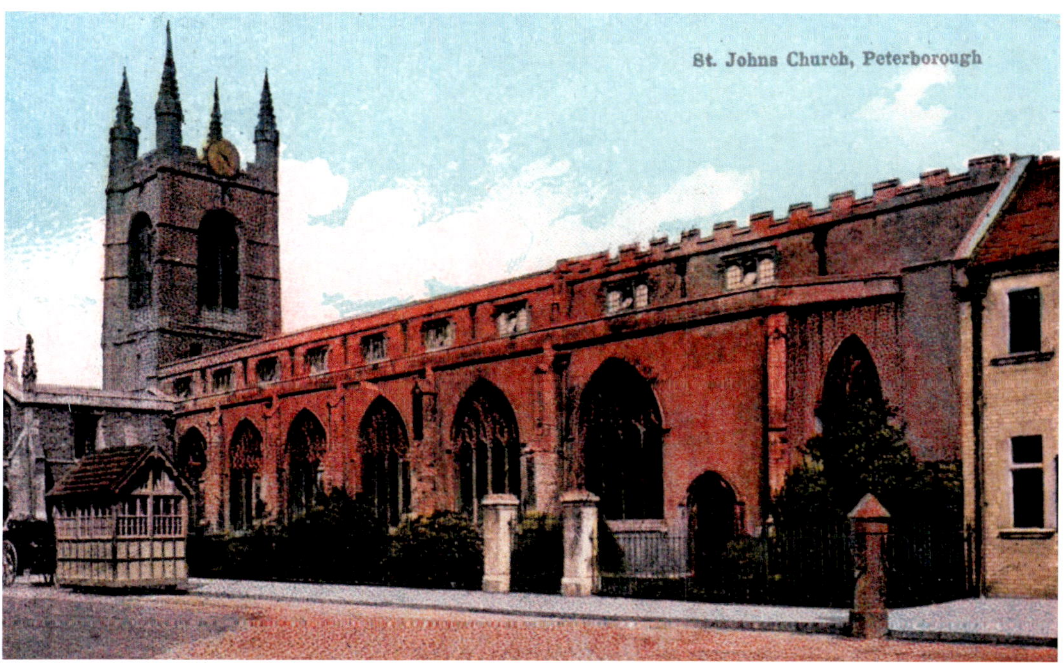

Water pump on roadside outside St John the Baptist's Church, *c.* 1905.

Gaunt's pump in Frog Hall Lane was the last and only pump in the city that did not run dry in 1868. A chap named Sheffield who lived in Frog Hall Lane used to take water from the pump in a tub on his donkey-pulled cart to supply people with water at a cost. He also used to gather up all the rubbish in the city.

Where All Souls' Catholic Church stands on the corner of Park Road and Geneva Street, there was a big reservoir belonging to Squire Tomlins. Until 1868 it was known to have never gone dry. There was another reservoir running alongside Craig Street which was supplied by water from Tom Lock's spring. A reservoir once existed at the site of the Hippodrome theatre on Broadway, extending to Swan's Pool, where livestock drank. It flowed through Minsters Yard to the river, but dried up during the drought.

Livestock got to a very low price as the grass was burnt up. Lambs fetched about 4–5s each and ewes 8–9s each. The harvest was all over in July. Wheat that could stand dry weather were good, but the rest of the crops, like barley, suffered.

The River Nene was so low that you could walk across it at almost any point as it was dry right up to Colman's Mill. Fish lay dead on the banks as hundreds were killed by the salt water and not fit to eat.

August brought heavy thunderstorms and rain. Seeds which were planted in April all came up and there was an abundance of winter feed and crops. They just grew as if they were in hothouses, and the quality and abundance was breathtaking.

Bibliography

Adrian Lyne (Tribute Entertainment, 2025)

Austin, G. D., *Peterborough Tramways* (1975)

'Century Story', *Peterborough Advertiser* (1854–1954)

Childers, John Walbanke, *Lord Orford's Voyage Round the Fens in 1774, the Journals of Thomas Roberts, George Farrington and Lord Orford* (2015)

DeLong, William, *Black Shuck: The Hellhound of the English Countryside* (1127)

Dufty, Arthur, *Peterborough New Town* (1969)

Entertainment USA (1983)

Gunton, Symon, *The Cathedral Church of Peterborough* (1686)

History, Topography, and Directory of Northamptonshire including the City & Diocese of Peterborough (1874)

'John Landen', *Encyclopaedia Britannica* (1911)

Karno, Fred, blog (January 2011)

Kelly's Directory (Peterborough, 1838, 1848, 1870, 1898, 1922, 1927, 1940, 1952, 1961, 1963)

Larrett, W. D., *A History of The King's School, Peterborough* (1966)

Mitchell, Neil, *The Streets of Peterborough* (2010)

Northampton Sites and Monuments Record

Padley, Priscilla, *Paten's Centenary, A History of Paten & Co. Ltd 1898–1998*

Peterborough, No. 218 of The 'Borough' Guides (Edward J. Burrow, 1904)

Pevsner, N., *The Buildings of England: Northamptonshire* (1961)

Phillipson, Laurel, *A Brief Guide to Museums in Cambridgeshire* (1986)

Sendall, Mike, obituary in *The Independent* (July 1999) and personal tribute from Sir Tim Berners-Lee, inventor of the world wide web (1999)

Rositzke, Harry A. (trans.), *The Peterborough Chronicle* (1951)

Sweeting, Revd W. D., *Historical and Architectural Notes on the Parish Churches In and Around Peterborough* (1868)

'The Peterborough Story', *Peterborough Evening Telegraph* (c. 1988)

Victoria County History IV

Webb, Leslie, *Some Peterborough Buildings* (1986)

Acknowledgements

In researching this book, we have deepened our knowledge of our great city, its people and places. We owe special thanks to the late Kathleen Church, Jack Gaunt, John and Jo Gillatt, Marina Jones, Harry Miles and daughter Jean Miles, Brian and Mary Rainey, and John Seeley.

Our gratitude also goes to fellow local historians Neil Mitchell, Rita McKenzie, Judy Bunten, Peter Waszak, Peter Clarkson, Brian White, and Stephen Perry, Trevor Pearce, Julie Nicholson and Dinah Watkins for their valuable support over the years. Special thanks to Adam Bowen for colourising some of our black-and-white images.